THE ARTILLERY OF THE PRESS

Its Influence on American Foreign Policy

THE ARTILLERY
OF THE PRESS

Its Influence on American Foreign Policy

---

by

JAMES RESTON

Published for the

COUNCIL ON FOREIGN RELATIONS

by

HARPER & ROW, PUBLISHERS

New York and Evanston

The Council on Foreign Relations is a nonprofit institution devoted to the study of political, economic, and strategic problems as related to American foreign policy. It takes no stand, expressed or implied, on American policy.

The authors of books published under the auspices of the Council are responsible for their statements of fact and expressions of opinion. The Council is responsible only for determining that they should be presented to the public.

For a list of Council publications see pages 113–116.

THE ARTILLERY OF THE PRESS:
ITS INFLUENCE ON AMERICAN FOREIGN POLICY

Copyright © 1966, 1967 by Council on Foreign Relations, Inc.
*All rights reserved, including the right to reproduce
this book or any portion thereof in any form.*
*For information, address Harper & Row, Publishers, Incorporated,
49 East 33rd Street, New York, N.Y. 10016*

FIRST EDITION

Library of Congress catalog card number: 67-11330
Printed in the United States of America
Published by Harper & Row, Publishers, Incorporated

B-R

1386279

IN MEMORY OF EDWARD JOHN NOBLE

The publication of this volume of The Elihu Root Lectures was aided by a grant from the Edward John Noble Foundation in memory of Mr. Noble and his interest in encouraging American leadership.

THE ELIHU ROOT LECTURES

INTRODUCTION

This book is based on three lectures given in the Elihu Root series before the members of the Council on Foreign Relations in New York City in 1966. It is an attempt to define and illustrate the problems of conducting American foreign policy in the last third of the twentieth century with a press and a Constitution whose traditions were formed in the last third of the eighteenth century. In particular, I have tried to make a few modest and, I hope, practical suggestions for improving the relations between reporters and officials rather than put forward ideal solutions which neither would be likely to accept.

I have called it *The Artillery of the Press,* borrowing a phrase Thomas Jefferson used in his second Inaugural Address. "The artillery of the press," he said, "has been levelled against us, charged with whatsoever its licentiousness could devise or dare. These abuses of an institution so important to freedom and science are deeply to be regretted, inasmuch as they tend to lessen its usefulness, and to sap its safety."

My theme is that the rising power of the United States in world affairs, and particularly of the American President, requires, not a more compliant press, but a relentless barrage of facts and criticism, as noisy but also as accurate as artillery fire. This means a less provincial, even a less nationalistic, press, because our job in this age, as I see it, is not to serve as cheerleaders for our side in the present world struggle but to help the largest possible number of people to see the realities of the changing and convulsive world in which American policy must operate. It also means a redefinition of what is "news," with more attention to the *causes* rather than merely the *effects* of international strife— at least by those American agencies, newspapers, and networks covering and influencing world affairs.

I began to think about this problem because of an unusual experience. In 1943, during one of the great crises of the Second World War, Arthur Hays Sulzberger, then publisher of *The New York Times,* went to Moscow on assignment by the United States government and the American Red Cross, and took me along. At that time, the German armies were outside Smolensk, and Moscow was under seige. In order to get there, we had to fly from New York south to Belém in Brazil, then across the South Atlantic to Ascension Island and Accra, and thence across Africa to the Sudan, Egypt, Iran and north through the back door to Moscow.

Though we were not on newspaper business at the time, we asked to see the editors of the official newspaper, *Pravda,* and were received with courtesy and shown around the *Pravda* offices. The directors took us to their offices, the mechanical departments, the housing for the printers and writers, and even the theater built especially for *Pravda* families. But one thing surprised us. There was no editorial room where the reporters gathered to report their findings and write their dispatches. We asked about this, since the "city room" is the heart of any American newspaper office. Our hosts did not understand, but the explanation soon became clear. The "news" was not produced in that building. The "reporters" were not reporters in the American sense of the word. The "news" came over wires from government offices somewhere else in Moscow. The "reporters" were technicians, processing what officials elsewhere decided should go in the paper.

I should have known this was true. In that brave and grim city at that moment when the German artillery was not far away, I could even believe in the necessity of a controlled press, but I was still startled by the thought that the press should be the instrument, rather than the critic, of the government. I have been fascinated by the different theories of the proper relationship between reporters and officials ever since.

In the twenty-three years since that first experience in Moscow, I have spent most of my time covering the conflict between these two quite different societies, and nowhere is the difference more apparent than in the Soviet assumption that the press must be controlled and the American assumption that it must be free. Time and again, in the struggles over Azerbaijan, Greece, Germany, Korea, the Congo, Cuba, and Viet Nam, it was clear that Moscow, with its controlled press, had many tactical advantages over Washington, which had to deal not only with the opposition of the Soviets but also with the skepticism of its own reporters.

American reporters worry about this dilemma between their obligation to the truth and their obligation to their country much more than is generally realized. They know that they often embarrass officials by reporting the facts, and even interfere with public policy occasionally, but they go on doing it because, somehow, the tradition of reporting the facts, no matter how much they hurt, is stronger than any other.

What is interesting is that most officials, no matter how embarrassed or irritated by the indiscreet or even dangerous disclosures of reporters, still defend—at least later in life after they leave public office—the right and even the duty of reporters to go on publishing as much of the truth as they can get, even if this causes the kind of problems these lectures were intended to analyze.

I am grateful to the Council on Foreign Relations for giving me the opportunity to talk about this problem; to John J. McCloy, former President of the World Bank and U.S. High Commissioner to Germany, who presided over the first of these lectures, and Douglas Dillon, former Under Secretary of State and Secretary of the Treasury, who served as chairman of the second and third, and to those members of the Council who still retain enough interest in these problems to endure lectures of this sort.

I am thinking of James B. Conant, Henry M. Wriston, Norman

Armour, Lewis Douglas, and Thomas K. Finletter as symbols of that remarkable generation of Americans who have labored with the problems of American foreign policy over the years. These men and many other members of the Council were born near the turn of the century. Thus they were influenced by the First World War, and worked in both public and private life on the historic transition from American isolation to American leadership in the world.

All of them have, at one time or another, been targets of "the artillery of the press," yet they have survived their wounds and retained not only an interest in the problem of reporters and officials but a determination to try to improve the relations between the men who make and the men who report the news.

I am grateful to them and to Ensign Craig Whitney of the U.S. Navy, my former associate on *The New York Times*, who helped with the research on this project; to my old friends and colleagues Ferdinand Kuhn and E. W. Kenworthy, who read the manuscript; and to my wife, Sally Fulton Reston, who, suffering through the production of these talks, and with no disrespect to Elihu Root, christened the following as the "root hog or die" lectures.

J. R.

Fiery Run, Virginia
December 24, 1966

CONTENTS

"Why should freedom of speech and freedom of press be allowed? Why should a government which is doing what it believes to be right allow itself to be criticized? It would not allow opposition by lethal weapons. Ideas are much more fatal things than guns. Why should any man be allowed to buy a printing press and disseminate pernicious opinions calculated to embarrass the government?"

—NIKOLAI LENIN, speech in Moscow, 1920

"The basis of our governments being the opinion of the people, the very first object should be to keep that right, and were it left to me to decide whether we should have a government without newspapers, or newspapers without a government, I should not hesitate a moment to choose the latter."

—THOMAS JEFFERSON, 1787

I

THE TUG
OF HISTORY

Do the People Know Best?

THE CONFLICT between the men who make and the men who report the news is as old as time. News may be true, but it is not truth, and reporters and officials seldom see it the same way. The first great event, or Man in the News, was Adam, and the accounts of his creation have been the source of controversy ever since. In the old days, the reporters or couriers of bad news were often put to the gallows; now they are given the Pulitzer Prize, but the conflict goes on.

The reasons are plain enough. We are changing the world faster than we can change ourselves. We are applying to the present the habits of the past. We are imposing on a transformed world the theories and assumptions that worked at home in another time, and nowhere does this clash of past and present, of theory and reality, seem more dramatic than in the application of American constitutional theory to the conduct of American foreign policy.

That theory is that the people know best. We deeply, almost instinctively, believe that the success of any group of people in dealing with their common problems rests on their knowledge and understanding of the problems to be solved, and on their intelligence, judgment, and character in meeting those problems. And the conclusion drawn from this is that the intelligence, judgment, and character of a majority of the people, if well informed, will probably produce more satisfactory solutions than any leader or small band of geniuses is likely to produce.

This is the background of what we need to analyze, for the conflict between officials and reporters is merely one expression of this wider constitutional theory of the relationship between opinion and policy. It is undoubtedly good as a guide to sinking a sewer or building a bridge or a school in a local community, but is it a sound way to conduct a foreign policy? Are the people getting adequate information to enable them to reach sound judgments on what to do about South Asia, or the Atlantic community, or the balance of payments, or China, or outer space? Is there any such information or any such people? And would enough of them pay attention and sustain a commercial newspaper or radio or television station that concentrated on these fundamental issues?

These questions raise the old problem of the people's right to be informed and the government's obligation to govern effectively, which sometimes means governing secretly. Two contemporary situations illustrate the dilemma. On the one hand, more than 400,000 Americans, most of them conscripts, are now fighting a war in Viet Nam. Most of them do not know how it started, and even many officials are extremely vague about how we got so deeply involved. It cannot be said that the people were well informed before their commitment to the battle, or even that their representatives in the Congress really debated the decision to wage this kind of war at the time of our involvement.

On the other hand, the President is now conducting that war as Commander in Chief, while television cameras on the battlefield record daily for vast television audiences some of the most brutal and agonizing scenes of the struggle.

In the first situation, there was so little information and so much executive authority that the President could do about what he pleased; and in the second, the people have so much information about the violent incidents of the war that it is questionable whether the President of a democratic country can really sustain his policy over a long period of time while the public is being invited to tune in on the eleven o'clock news and see Johnny killed. Something is obviously out of balance here. When a nation can conscript its men to fight a war they know little about and then wage that war on the television screens of the homes of the fighting men, the relationship between public opinion and public policy surely needs analysis.

Also, it should be analyzed down in the pit where both officials and reporters operate under the tyranny of fact, deadline, and decision. Academic monographs on ideal reporters and officials in a perfect world are not very helpful. The President has no choice between dealing with the military situation and the political tradition. He has to deal with both. Similarly, the owners and managers of newspapers and radio and television stations are not likely to spend more time thinking about their duty than about their economic security. I happen to believe that they would probably be better off if they thought more about their duty and less about their security, but that is not the way it is, and therefore it is probably more useful to try to understand the practical everyday conflict between reporters and officials and how it developed.

The Conflict of Tradition

The United States had a press before it had a foreign policy. This explains a large part of the tension between its reporters and its officials even today. The American press was telling the country and the world where to get off before there was a State Department. The eighteenth-century American pamphleteers not only helped write the Constitution, but thought—with considerable justification—that they created the Union. They believed that government power was potentially if not inevitably wicked and had to be watched, especially when applied in secret and abroad, and they wrote the rules so that the press would be among the watchers.

The Founding Fathers were quite dogmatic about this. They not only denied that government had the power to censor the press—as had the British government from which they had just declared their independence—but wrote into the first article of the Bill of Rights a flat prohibition against Congressional regulation of the press, and even assumed the opposite: that the press would censor the government. "No government ought to be without censors," Jefferson wrote to President Washington in 1792, "and where the press is free, no one ever will." Although Jefferson insisted the papers should be held responsible for published falsehood, he and his colleagues agreed in general that the best way for the press to serve the country was to criticize it, and something of this same pugnacious spirit remains in our newspaper offices today.

The American diplomat, while part of this same tradition, was greatly influenced by the British view that foreign policy was a subject for professionals, not amateurs, and that newspaper reporters, while often amusing fellows, were an irritation if not a danger. The *Encyclopaedia Britannica,* expressing a typical British view of reporters, begins its description of "Journalism and Journalists" as follows: "Though the qualifications and status of Clergymen, Physicians, and members of many other professions are definite, the Journalist continues to follow an indeterminate calling with neither qualifications nor status precisely defined." This low view of the "indeterminate calling" has never been wholly absent from the corridors of the State Department.

Also, the American diplomat before World War II was trained in the days of our isolation to be a silent observer of world affairs. He was as discreet as a priest. He was supposed to know everything and to tell nothing. He ate in places with tablecloths and spoke French. Even in America, let alone Britain, your ideal State Department man was as handsome as Joseph Grew and as elegant as Dean Acheson, and as prudent as both.

In contrast, the American reporter, circa 1930, was a very gabby and even rakish character, who took pleasure in his own caricature as a romantic roughneck, part cop and part Robin Hood. Stanley Walker, the famous city editor of the tragic *New York Herald Tribune,* once spoofed him as follows:

"What makes a good newspaperman? The answer is easy. He knows everything. He is aware not only of what goes on in the world today, but his brain is a repository of the accumulated wisdom of the ages. Moreover, he is somewhat psychic, and is able to sense what the news will be tomorrow, and next month, and even next year. He writes prose that is not only crisp but graceful. He can perform any job in journalism. He is not only handsome, but he has the physical stamina which enables him to perform great feats of energy. He can go for nights on end without sleep. He dresses well and talks with charm. Men admire him; women adore him; tycoons and statesmen are happy to share their secrets with him. He takes a drink but never gets drunk. He is good to his family, if any. He hates lies and meanness and sham, but keeps his temper. He is loyal to his paper and to what he looks upon as his profession; whether it is a profession, or merely a craft, he resents attempts to debase it. When he dies, a lot of people are sorry, and some of them remember him for several days."

This, of course, was charming nonsense, but the reporter of that day was certainly different from his counterpart of the 1960s. He was usually trained in the police court, the county courthouse, or, as in my own case, the sports press box (where, incidentally, you had the consolation of knowing who had won at the end of the day). He was not discreet, but skeptical and often even impertinent. His general view of public officials was that they were probably up to something bad, which the Founding Fathers had somehow appointed him personally to expose.

There were, of course, in the period between the two world wars some cultivated American foreign correspondents, who carried umbrellas and even read books, but my own introduction into foreign correspondence was probably more typical of the period. I went to London in 1937, primarily to cover the tennis matches at Wimbledon, the international golf tournaments, the Irish sweepstakes and the Grand National steeplechase at Aintree. My first assignment was to accompany the American Ryder Cup professional golf team across the Atlantic, and I still count it as a great event that on the way over I roomed with Sam Snead, the rookie sensation of the day. Nevertheless, though I vividly remember studying the map of Europe on the boat and trying to puzzle out the difference between the Balkans and the Baltic states, within two months I was covering the Foreign Office in London for the largest American news agency, the Associated Press.

This personal reference may not be very reassuring, but it is not wholly irrelevant. In its sudden transformation from isolation to leader of a world-wide coalition of nations, America is still a nation of amateurs. Even today, almost everybody in a position of power or influence in Washington is surprised to find himself where he is. This may not be true of the members of the Joint Chiefs of Staff and some U.S. ambassadors in major embassies, who came out of professional military academies and the Foreign Service, but it is true of every member of the President's cabinet. And certainly, this amateurishness was an accurate symbol of the time and transition.

Too Much and Too Soon

The relations between press and government in the field of foreign policy are merely a dramatic illustration of this wider American problem. It is not only the relations between journalism and diplomacy that are in a state of bewildering transition in the 1960s, but also the relations between President and Vice President, White House and Capitol Hill, Federal government and state government, governor and mayor, management and labor, church and parishioner, university and student, and even parent and child.

The British had five generations in which to adjust their private attitudes and public institutions to their growing imperial responsibilities in the world. They had time to mobilize the Scottish nanny and the British public school, without which they could never have reconciled the private and public responsibilities of their military and diplomatic services. They were able to maintain their imperial responsibilities, often by dubious and even brutal means, without having to worry about day-to-day reporting of their actions in Fleet Street. But the United States did not have time to adjust its attitudes and its national institutions to its world responsibilities, and the conflict between the press and foreign policy is merely one illustration of this devilish race with the pace of history.

The American reporter of my generation was brought up to believe in the cocky frontier tradition of "publish and be damned," but the American diplomat of the same age quickly came to believe that if he helped you to publish the facts, *he* was likely to be damned, and this was only one of the conflicts that soon developed between the government and the press.

The conduct of foreign policy is a process that never ends; the production of a newspaper or a television news program is a miracle that has to be accomplished somehow on the split second. Former Secretary of State Dean Acheson took up furniture-making because, as he once explained to me, "When I finish making a table I know where I am: it is not like a foreign policy; I don't have to wait twenty-five years to see how the thing comes out."

It is not easy in a democracy to reconcile the habits of one profession with the habits of another. John Foster Dulles was a lawyer and a moralist. Everything in his background and legal training tended to make him think in terms of good and evil, victory and defeat, precedents and judgments. He divided foreign policy into separate cases, applied precedents that worked in Europe to wholly different conditions in Asia, and demonstrated in the process that training in one field is not necessarily applicable to another.

Journalism and foreign policy in America are even harder to reconcile. The Secretary of State must think in generations and continents, but the reporter thinks in "stories," in "minutes," and often in "fragments." One profession is quiet, the other noisy; one slow, the other fast; one precise, the other imprecise. What makes their relationship even more difficult is that they are stuck with one another.

They are married without the possibility of divorce, separation, or even an occasional period of quiet. The government is always acting and the press is always blabbing and criticizing, and what makes this alliance even more galling is that it is unequal.

Even in these days when there is a television studio in the basement of the White House, the reporter is usually the first bearer of the news. He tells what is done by the Chief Magistrate and sometimes what is not done. He tells it to the people, who have the power to fire the Chief Magistrate. If he does not tell the truth, *he* is in trouble; if he does tell the truth, very often the Chief Magistrate is in even more trouble. This does not contribute much to their mutual affection. They are both working in a strange situation, largely in accordance with their traditions of the past; and this is the root of the tension, which is being aggravated by the conflict of old traditions and new complexities.

II

THE TYRANNY
OF TECHNIQUES

How the Press Behaves

ONE of the oddities of this time is the tendency to analyze the press—or what has unfortunately come to be called "the mass media"—as if it were some monumental and even monolithic institution like the Roman Catholic Church. When I bummed home on graduation day 1932 from the University of Illinois to join the sports department of the Springfield, Ohio, *Daily News* at ten dollars a week, the press was discussed mainly in saloons as a nuisance; now it is dissected in drawing rooms and universities as a menace. Solemn and intelligent men, amateur sociologists all, actually gather from many countries these days, usually at the expense of the Ford Foundation, and ponder darkly how democracy can survive with this monster in its midst.

Let us add a few facts to this melancholy view. The American press, which takes in everything from *The New York Times* to the Sycamore, Illinois, *True Republican* and the *Fauquier Democrat* of Warrenton, Virginia, is a comparatively small and diverse institution operating in a very large world. Press, radio, and television in the United States employ about 600,000 people. Of these, the number who actually write and edit the news is only about 60,000, and the nearest that most of them get to the intractable mysteries of foreign policy is when some ambassador comes to town and talks to the local Rotary Club.

There are actually only a few hundred American reporters, editors, and commentators dealing primarily with foreign-policy questions all over the world, and those with the largest newspaper circulation are not the well-known commentators but the news agency reporters who provide most of the copy for most daily American newspapers and the radio and television stations as well.

Two points of history and geography are relevant to an understanding of the American news agency. Unlike Reuters in Britain, Havas in France, and Wolff in Germany, the original American news agency, the Associated Press, was created not for private profit or government convenience but as a nonprofit cooperative association to serve the newspapers that shared the costs. This had some significance. The Associated Press was founded in 1848, when newspapers were much more partisan and personal than they are today; but since it had to serve editors of wholly different and conflicting views on domestic and foreign policy, it had to be as impartial, nonpartisan, and unbiased as possible. The result was that mutual distrust among American newspapers created the most accurate and trustworthy source of spot news the world has ever seen, and with the advent of a second American world-wide news agency, now called United Press International, competition increased both the flow and the accuracy of the news.

The geographical point is more interesting and less encouraging. The American news agencies have to serve a vast continental country covering four different time zones, with some parts facing on the Pacific and some on the Atlantic, some looking north and some south, some living in Arctic and some in tropical climates. Accordingly, news has to be written so that a news story on, say, international trade has to be filed at length for maritime cities interested in international commerce and in brief for agricultural towns concerned primarily with the price of corn. And vice versa. A decision in Washington to encourage and finance the production of soybeans and rice to meet the threat of famine in Asia has to be written in detail for newspapers and radio stations in areas that produce rice and soybeans, but cut down for newspapers in Alaska or New York City which have no local interest in either crop.

This may seem remote, but it is highly relevant to the question of how the American people hear about the world. For to serve newspapers and radio and television stations which cannot afford their own correspondents everywhere—which means almost all of them—the news agencies had to devise a technique of writing the news so that each story could be adapted to the diverse needs and interests of widely varied communities.

Accordingly, they invented the "headline" or "all-purpose" agency news story which could be published at length in the large city papers, or cut in half for those in the middle-sized towns, or even reduced to a paragraph for the very small papers. This solution to a technical problem had results that nobody in the Associated Press or United Press International intended and certainly nobody in the State Department wanted. For it tended to sharpen and inflate the news. It created a tradition of putting the most dramatic fact in the story first—the hot angle—and then following it with paragraphs of decreasing importance. Thus it encouraged not a balanced but a startling, even a breathless, presentation of the news, featuring the flaming lead and the big headline.

This was adequate for the news of wrecks, murders, or football games, but was a limiting and distorting technique as news of foreign policy became more important and more complicated. It is easy to write an account of a sports event in such a way that it can be sent out on the wires in great detail or cut to a sentence —after all, the main thing is who won and who lost—but a Senate debate on U.S. relations with China, though important to a reader's understanding of the future, cannot be reduced to a paragraph without leaving the reader in ignorance of what really happened.

The Associated Press, especially when under the direction of wide-minded professional reporters like Wes Gallagher and Alan Gould, has made great progress in supplementing its spot-news file with special reports by experienced and reflective men like John Hightower. But the tyranny of time and geography is still a major agency problem, and it is hard to overestimate its importance in any study of the total effect of foreign news on American opinion.

Not only do the news agency reports reach more readers and

listeners than all the news services of all the large papers combined, but they greatly influence the editors of even the largest newspapers and networks. The news agencies are in first with the news. They provide the editors with simple headlines (that are often simpler than the truth); and since they make the first impression on the editors, the tendency of these editors, even on some of the best papers, is to suggest or even to insist that their own reporters, who have more time for reflecting and composing than the Associated Press and United Press International reporters have, follow the lead of the agency dispatches.

These technicalities may be tiresome to the reader but they are also vital. In the first place, the news agencies are the really important schools of journalism in America. Most of the leading reporters on the big newspapers are trained there in the who-what-where-when-and-why techniques of the agencies, and the trouble with the technique is that the "why," which is first in the understanding of the day's news, comes last on the list, and often gets left out altogether.

Also, the news agency is especially vulnerable to the cult of objectivity, which has done so much in the last generation to confuse "news" with truth. Since it serves newspapers of varying political opinions, the agency is not so vulnerable to the old sin of slanting the news. A Republican or a Democratic paper can print all the news that fits its political bias and ignore or cut and hide all the news that doesn't, but not a news agency filing information to both Republican and Democratic, isolationist or internationalist papers. The news agency led the way in what was called "objective reporting," which for a long time came to mean that "news" was anything any big-shot said. If Senator Joseph McCarthy of Wisconsin said that there were over one hundred card-carrying Communists in the State Department, out it would go on the wires regardless of whether or not what the Senator said was true. And the newspapers not only published and repeated endlessly rubbish of this kind, but fell into the same habit of following the technique themselves, all in the name of "objectivity."

"Our rut of routine and formulae in defining, writing, and displaying the news . . . were our tools and they have all but become our masters," Eric Sevareid observed in 1953. "Our rigid formulae of so-called objectivity . . . have given the lie the same prominence and impact that truth is given; they have elevated the influence of fools to that of wise men; the ignorant to the level of the learned; the evil to the level of the good."

Fortunately, this habit of shoveling unchecked charges into the papers has declined in recent years, partly because Soviet officials decided they could easily use the "anything's news" technique as an instrument of their propaganda. Lately, the papers and the agencies have resorted to separate "news analysis" articles to decontaminate this kind of poison, but the problem is not solved, and it is not easy to solve. For a lie in a front-page dispatch is much more powerful than a correcting truth back inside the paper or on the editorial page. The newspaper cannot very well follow the wry suggestion of the late Elmer Davis and print on page one: "For the truth about what you read below, see the editorial page." Somehow, what is said on the front page has to be put into the perspective of truth, to the best of the reporter's and editor's capacity to ascertain the truth; but this is difficult, for whoever undertakes to correct error takes the risk and responsibility of committing error on the other side.

Nevertheless, a new generation of American reporters and editors, better educated and more interested in being right than being first with the news, and much more concerned with the explanation of events, is slowly improving the perspective of the papers and the networks; but the influence of history and geography and dramatic paper-selling techniques is still with us, and new complications are adding to the problem.

The New Complications

Everybody in Washington is now plagued by numbers: more nations to deal with; more departments and agencies along the Potomac; more centers of power over foreign policy in the

Pentagon and the White House; more private advisers to the President in the law and newspaper offices of Washington and even in the Supreme Court building; more ambassadors to receive and dinners and "national days" to attend; more visiting dignitaries seeking aid and publicity; more bills and reports and committee hearings and visiting voters on Capitol Hill; more advisory committees on technical and scientific matters; more back-door visits to the White House that the reporters know nothing about.

How is it all to be reported? What should or should not be reported? Who is making the critical recommendations—responsible, visible officials or private, invisible friends of the President? In this new turbulent world of specialists on science, economics, and the politics and psychology of Asia, of special emissaries and secret missions, of diplomacy by transoceanic telephone and "hot lines" to Moscow, everybody finds himself in a new and strange situation.

Who decides whether it is prudent or foolish to embark on a $30 billion project to build an antiballistic missile system? What are the facts, and who decides what facts are critical, and who picks the people who pick the facts? In this maze, the Secretaries of State and Defense, the new technical advisers, and the old ambassadors are never quite sure where their responsibility starts and ends. Even some of the most prominent Congressmen are not quite sure of their role. The Chairman of the Senate Armed Services Committee may find himself invited in private to recommend a policy involving new risks of a larger war, while the Chairman of the Foreign Relations Committee may find himself condemned by the White House for expressing opposition to White House policy on the floor of the Senate.

The State Department's Director of Intelligence and Research, Thomas L. Hughes, taking a cue from C. P. Snow, thinks he has discovered in Washington "the two cultures" of American foreign policy. The new technicians at the Pentagon, the new scientific experts at the Rand Corporation and other "think tanks," and the new industry-oriented advisers outside the government are competing for influence over foreign policy with the old traditional advisers concerned with the more humanistic intangibles of foreign politics, skepticism, and belief.

"Today," Hughes observes, "the personal dimension of foreign affairs is becoming over-powering. The burden of everybody else's insatiable involvement is almost unsupportable for the old time foreign affairs professional . . . Today foreign policy is the pre-occupation of nearly everyone who is not officially assigned to it, from the Secretary of the Interior to the Mayor of Willimantic. All cabinet members, all governors, all congressmen, all university presidents, most mayors, all important business and labor leaders, professors, ministers, farmers, journalists, students, safari goers, and most other participants in the Affluent Society are volunteer-ing to help." Poor man—he foresees the ultimate deprofessionaliza-tion of foreign policy, and, of course, he has a point.

The Washington press corps, being more outside than Hughes is, has the same problem, only worse, for it has to worry not only about the government's size and confusion but about its own size and confusion as well. When I started covering the State Depart-ment for *The New York Times* in 1941, Secretary of State Hull saw the journalistic "regulars" every weekday in his office. There were about ten of us then. A generation later, when my son Richard began covering the State Department for the *Los Angeles Times*, the Secretary of State had to meet the reporters in an auditorium where everybody was wired for sound.

Mr. Hull could explain his policies, often in the most vivid Tennessee mountain language, read from the diplomatic cables if he felt like it, and indicate, with full assurance that his con-fidences would be respected, what was on the record and what had to be off the record.

It is still possible, of course, to have private communications between responsible officials and responsible reporters, but this has to be done on an individual basis or with only a few reporters present. This puts one more burden on American officials, who are now dealing with more problems all over the world, more ambassadors in a swollen diplomatic corps, more dinners—and what dinners!—and more demands from more committees of the

Congress for more explanations of things that are often beyond explanation.

The change in the nature of war has also greatly complicated the problem of reconciling the traditions of reporters and government. The nation is engaged in an underground war, an economic war, and an intelligence war on every continent of the earth—and not only there but in the heavens above the earth where satellites spin through outer space photographing potentially hostile nations, and in caves below the earth where sensitive instruments watch for underground explosions and other signs of military experimentation.

This requires a vast American secret service operation in the armed services, the State Department, and the Central Intelligence Agency. It is obviously essential in such a world. It is paid for with public funds. What it costs and what all it does—abroad as well as in research projects in our own universities—are not disclosed. Not only is this necessary, but it is something comparatively new and puzzling in American life, at least on the present scale. The old tradition of the American press was that anything a government hides, except during open and declared war, was wrong, probably wicked, and therefore should be exposed; but a press demanding unlimited freedom for this principle today could in many cases risk the nation's security. Yet the problem cannot be solved simply by saying that the operations of the intelligence services of the government are none of the public's business.

I knew for over a year that the United States was flying high-altitude planes (the U-2) over the Soviet Union from a base in Pakistan to photograph military and particularly missile activities and bases, but *The New York Times* did not publish this fact until one of the planes was shot down in 1960. Was this a correct judgment? I think it was, but in other circumstances the press is criticized for not printing intelligence and even military information.

For example, Arthur Schlesinger, Jr., the historian who served as an assistant to President John F. Kennedy, thinks that less responsibility—in fact, pitiless publicity—on the part of the press before the invasion of Cuba at the Bay of Pigs might have saved the nation from the consequences of that fiasco. After the event, but not before, President Kennedy agreed.

On the other hand, premature publication of the movement of American ships and men to intercept the Soviet ships bringing missiles to Havana in the second Cuban crisis of 1962 could easily have interfered with what proved to be an essential and spectacularly successful exercise of American power and diplomacy.

Responsible officials and news reporters and executives have not been able to resolve this new intelligence problem. There is no guiding principle that will cover all cases, yet it is clear in this time of half-war and half-peace that the old principle of publish-and-be-damned, while very romantic, bold and hairy, can often damage the national interest. And there are other fields in which the responsibility of the press is increasing with the world power of the nation.

The American press, radio, and television, for example, are no longer merely national institutions catering to a national audience. Like the rest of American Big Business, they are distributing their services all over the world. News reports of the Associated Press, United Press International, *The New York Times*, the *Washington Post* and the *Los Angeles Times* are being published now on every continent. The same is true of the weekly news magazines, *Time* and *Newsweek*. This expanded distribution raises new and sometimes unexpected problems.

If *Time* magazine does a cover-story on one of the leaders of Viet Nam, for example, the other competing leaders tend to regard this as undue influence on the internal political and personal struggle within that country. Reading these magazines and news reports abroad, officials of other countries often complain that American news of their affairs is unfair or, what is often worse, ignored. An inaccuracy about foreign affairs in the American press which might have been overlooked before World War II now becomes a big issue in foreign capitals within a matter of hours and often leads to official protests in Washington. This is another complication for both officials and reporters.

There is a further effect of this international influence. An American press that tends to concentrate on the violence and disputes within the United States inevitably if unconsciously gives a rather negative picture of this country overseas, and the transmission of television broadcasts by satellite across the oceans is not likely to decrease this problem.

News written in the United States for a national audience that understands the national institutions, habits, and personalities— that does not expect the President and the Chairman of the Foreign Relations Committee to take the same line—does not always seem the same when read by overseas audiences that do not have the same background. George V. Ferguson, editor of the *Montreal Star*, makes the point quite sharply. "To the outside eye," he tells us, "the first impression is one of unending confusion and disorder. Discordant voices are raised on every side. The debates seem to proceed in a series of vast and unregulated explosions. It is a process which encourages extremes, and, as public opinion slowly forms, the extreme voices are those most loudly and frequently heard. The impression is one of Babel in its more inchoate moments, and, from day to day, as one voice and then another makes itself most clearly heard in the tumult, the untrained outsider is likely to conclude that a people so inherently confused and unstable has only itself to blame for the disasters that are bound to pursue it." Mr. Ferguson, being a well-informed Canadian and knowing our habits, makes allowance for our exuberance, but obviously less informed readers overseas do not.

All these complications are the natural, perhaps the inevitable, result of events moving more quickly than men and institutions can change. The tug of history, the influence of geography, the tyranny of old journalistic techniques, the problems of science, the sensitive dilemmas of underground war, and the growth and expansion of journalism in the world—all this sometimes seems, as Henry Thoreau said of the first railroad train, to be merely "wickedness going faster," and it creates problems which are not easy to solve.

III

PUBLISH
AND BE DAMNED?

The Practical Dilemmas

THE HISTORICAL, geographical, and technical problems discussed in preceding chapters create some awkward and even dangerous situations for everybody concerned. Officials and newsmen may try in their own ways to solve them, but if they can't they still have to live in their competitive worlds. The pressures of world events, the insistent inquiries of the Congress, and the uncertainties of the next election all weigh on the President and his associates. The news agencies, the radio and television networks, the newspapers, and the news magazines are all in fierce commercial competition with one another. All reporters may reflect after working hours on a more ideal world, but they have to live and work in the world as it is.

A few illustrations may help clarify the consequences. Perhaps the first critical American decision in the Viet Nam war came not during President Johnson's Administration but during his predecessor's when, late in 1961, President Kennedy decided to raise the American "presence" in Viet Nam from a few hundred military "advisers" to a military force of over 15,000 men. At that time, as we learned much later, the Under Secretary of State of the day, George W. Ball, opposed the move on the ground that if the United States committed that many men, it would commit the prestige of the United States, change the character of the war, and make withdrawal from the conflict very difficult.

He raised the central question in a meeting with Secretary of State Dean Rusk and Secretary of Defense Robert S. McNamara.

With this increase, he said, we are committing the prestige of the United States to the war. This may take as many as 300,000 Americans to achieve a military solution. "Are we prepared to see it through on this scale?" Ball said he was not. Rusk and McNamara both conceded that Ball's question was fair but also said yes, they were prepared to see it through. But the American people were not told that. The decision was seen by the public as a modest increase of the noncombatant American force, signifying no significant change in American policy; and, of course, the escalation went on from there, one "modest" increase after another until more than 400,000 Americans were fighting not only in South but over North Viet Nam.

In retrospect, this seems like a willful deception. I think the force was increased step by step over the years almost by stealth, but this is not the place to argue that. The purpose here is merely to illustrate the position of the official, the reporter, and the public in such a situation. Actually, there was no willful deception at the start. In the first place, all the officials concerned, President Kennedy, Rusk, McNamara, and Ball, hoped that the first increase to 15,000 men would stabilize the situation. They agreed about the risk but hoped to avoid the consequences.

Also, President Kennedy did not at that point make the basic policy decision that Viet Nam was "vital" to the security of the United States or that he was prepared to commit very large forces to see the thing through. It is easy to guess, however, what the reporters would have written if they had been told at the time the background of the important discussion of Rusk, McNamara, and Ball. They would certainly have written that the United States had decided to increase its force to 15,000, that this might lead to a commitment of as many as 300,000, and that there was a dispute among the President's top advisers about taking such a risk. Not wanting such a startling news story to go out, not even being sure that this would be the result of the action, the officials put out only a part of the story. No reporter managed to hear about the rest until much later, and the people were not informed about the risk they later had to redeem at the cost of many lives and of a war budget that eventually reached almost $2 billion a month.

During the Eisenhower Administration a comparable decision involving Viet Nam came to a quite different conclusion. In 1954, the French were in a critical battle against the Vietnamese Communists at Dienbienphu. The French asked for American air support, and they were supported by Secretary of State Dulles and the Chairman of the Joint Chiefs of Staff, Admiral Radford, both of whom believed Viet Nam to be "vital" to the security interests of the United States. Congressional leaders were called to the State Department for consultation, and the decisive opposition came from the Chairman of the Senate Armed Services Committee, Richard Russell of Georgia, and the Majority Leader of the Senate at the time, Lyndon B. Johnson of Texas. Again, what was "vital" or not vital to the nation was not really the subject of much public debate. Eisenhower sided with Johnson, who was later to assume the Presidency and fulfill Ball's melancholy prediction.

Governments, even in these days, are therefore not beyond taking risks which they do not confide to the people who have to pay the consequences. Nor do officials hesitate to mislead the people by withholding vital information already known to the enemy. For example, the United States government under President Johnson told the country in 1966 that it was renewing the bombing of North Viet Nam because the enemy had reinforced its fighting units in South Viet Nam during the lull in the bombing. What it did not disclose was that our government had itself reinforced the American expeditionary force there during the pause by many more men than the enemy sent into the South.

The conflict between officials and reporters comes up in other ways. For example, in 1955, President Eisenhower and Secretary of State Dulles decided that it might be useful to have a talk with the leaders of the Soviet Union at Geneva, and especially with Nikita Khrushchev, who had not yet become Premier but was reported to be making progress to the top and to favor a more conciliatory policy toward Washington. For diplomatic reasons, Mr. Eisenhower and Mr. Dulles determined in advance to take a friendly attitude toward the Soviet leaders and to create, if possible, a feeling in the world that the United States and the Soviet Union were composing their differences.

Even so fair and professional a diplomat as Ambassador Charles E. Bohlen, who served as the American spokesman at that conference, was obliged to stick to the official line that the conversations were going well. Meanwhile, Secretary Dulles and the Soviet Foreign Minister, Vyacheslav Molotov, were differing quite violently behind the scenes on almost every topic they discussed. The friendly statements were put out, but the substantive differences were not. The reporters, however, found out what was really happening in the Dulles-Molotov talks and reported the differences. They told the truth, but, as Eisenhower and Dulles saw it, they ruined the diplomatic intent of the mission.

The Kennedy-Khrushchev summit meeting at Vienna in 1961 was much the same. Again the official communiqués gave the impression that the talks had been "useful"—communiqués always do—but the fact was that it was a shouting match over Berlin and Germany most of the time, which led soon after to a decision by Kennedy to increase the military budget by $6 billion and send an additional American division to Germany. In fairness to Kennedy, it must be added that he told this reporter precisely what had happened a few minutes after the last meeting with Khrushchev; in this instance, the public did get the truth.

In some cases, the zeal of the press often puts officials in difficult situations that interfere with their legitimate official plans and lead to error, embarrassment, or worse. For example, in 1966 there was considerable opposition in Allied countries to the American war effort in Southeast Asia. There was also a genuine will on the part of President Johnson to try to get a negotiated settlement of that war through the intercession of some of the Allied countries. Failing to achieve this through diplomatic channels, the President and his aides debated at some length the advisability of the President going abroad to discuss the problem with some of the world leaders; but the public opposition of some peace groups in most

Allied countries was such that he hesitated to visit the major foreign capitals lest he be the subject of demonstrations in opposition to his Viet Nam policy. The problem here was not that the general public in Allied countries would have demonstrated against him, but that even a few demonstrators scuffling with the police and security officers would have provided news photographs certain to be used for effective propaganda and given the enemy the impression that the opposition to President Johnson was perhaps even more serious than it actually was. As a result, some of the trips discussed early in the year were abandoned.

Another example: News reports of events overseas usually travel faster than official reports, which have to be coded and decoded, and this sometimes causes problems. For example, Douglass Cater, in his excellent book, *The Fourth Branch of Government*, recalls an incident in November of 1951 when a report was published in the press about a bid by the Chinese Communists for a negotiated settlement of the Formosa controversy with the United States. The Secretary of State was away from Washington at the time, and the Under Secretary was in charge. Reporters naturally pressed him hard for a reply, but he had not yet received an official report of the incident. Nevertheless, knowing the report had been widely distributed throughout the United States and not wanting the Communists to have a propaganda advantage over the weekend, the Under Secretary dismissed the offer as mere propaganda, forcing the Secretary of State, on his return, to try to correct the blunder. Here was a case, not of the official refusing to cooperate with the reporters, but of his cooperating too much and too soon under their pressure.

There are many cases where officials and reporters are simply not able to agree about what should and should not be published. A vast increase in the use of electronic listening devices followed the invention of atomic weapons and intercontinental missiles. The United States, during the Administration of President Eisenhower, charged the Soviet Union with installing a miniature radio transmitting device back of the Great Seal of the United States in the Embassy in Moscow. Later, the United States was caught tapping the telephones of the Dominican Republic's Embassy in Washington. This was discovered by Drew Pearson and *The New York Times,* and the facts were published. In this case, the newspapers believed the secret use of these devices was getting out of hand, but the State Department's top officials felt that the papers not only interfered with the collection of important security information, but, by disclosing the truth in the Dominican case, made every other foreign embassy in Washington suspicious that its phones were tapped as well.

The Problems of Speculation

Speculative stories in the papers on what is being discussed or considered by officials in private often lead to trouble, and yet there are two sides to this. For example, at the height of the Soviet diplomatic and military pressure on Yugoslavia shortly after the Second World War, there was a series of urgent and secret meetings in Washington on what action the United States and Britain would take in the event of an armed attack on Yugoslavia. One reporter, at the peak of the crisis, published a report that Washington and London had decided that although they would give some aid to Yugoslavia if war broke out, they definitely would not go to war themselves against the Soviet Union in such a conflict. This naturally was interpreted by the Yugoslavs as an invitation to the Soviets to attack, and it was condemned in Washington, not because it was inaccurate—it happened to be true—but because it was a rash and senseless bit of reporting enterprise, disclosing information that was not essential to the American public, but highly useful to the Soviets and dangerous to the Yugoslavs.

On the other hand—such being the difficulty of defining general guiding principles in this field—failure on the part of reporters to publish private government information about what is being discussed and decided inside the government can often damage the national interest. The reporters knew all about the Kennedy Administration's plans to help mount an invasion against Cuba at the Bay of Pigs. Some papers reported what was afoot, others didn't; but after the invasion failed, President Kennedy told Turner Catledge, then managing editor of *The New York Times*, that he wished the press had disclosed much more information than we did. In that event, he remarked, the American people might have forced cancellation of one of the most embarrassing American military and diplomatic adventures of the century.

The Presidential news conference, so popular with reporters, also provides illustrations of the dangers of applying to one period of history the information techniques of another. Most of the time, it is a very useful institution. The President is not in the same position as the Prime Minister of a parliamentary democracy. He is not obliged to answer personally the inquiries of the political opposition. He may choose to invite their questions, as many Presidents have done in private meetings at the White House, but there is nothing in the Constitution that forces him to do so. Thus, with the development of television, speech-writing "ghosts," and tele-prompters that make a skillful politician look as if he is talking extemporaneously when he is merely reading somebody else's words, it is increasingly possible for a President to hide his real abilities, or lack thereof, behind a screen of words and thoughts not his own. Especially is this so if he is a good actor. The Presidential news conference was intended to minimize the possibilities of such deception and to provide a forum for the President, not mainly to put out his written statements, but to reply to questions on his stewardship and hear inquiries on some problems that might, in so vast a country, have escaped his attention.

In this sense, the White House press conference, started in the days of the nation's isolation, is an extremely useful device. But it varies in accordance with the ability of the President to express himself, and, unless handled with great skill in the delicate field of international relations, it can lead to dangerous imprecisions, particularly if the President is tired, which in these strenuous days happens a good deal of the time.

"The Horrors of Vagueness"

The British writer and diplomat Harold Nicolson, who has studied the problem of officials and the press from the diplomat's point of view, reaches the conclusion that nothing leads to more trouble in international relations than the cumulative exhaustion of endless work, and the imprecision which inevitably attends the extemporaneous open discussion of great questions by tired minds. Under the strain of incessant overwork, he believes, the imaginative and creative qualities of even the most muscular of human brains are apt to flag: more and more does the exhausted mind tend to concentrate upon the narrower circle of immediate detail; less and less does it aspire to those wider circles of vision which, once entered upon, must entail further discussion, further mental effort. In time, these "ordeals of exhaustion" lead to an aptitude for the superficial rather than for the essential, for the expedient in preference to the awkward, and for the improvised as an escape from the pondered.

"Some experience and much study of international negotiation," Nicolson wrote in *Peacemaking—1919*, "have left me with one abiding conviction . . . : The essential to good diplomacy is precision. The main enemy of good diplomacy is imprecision. It is for this reason that I have endeavored in this book to convey an impression of the horrors of vagueness. . . . Openness, in all such matters, leads to imprecision. No statesman is prepared in advance and in the open to bind himself to a precise policy. An imprecise policy means no policy at all. It means aspiration only."

How startling it is to see the lessons of the past, vividly defined, so often ignored, in our own time. Franklin Roosevelt was able to get away with casual talk in his press conferences. There was a kind of chirpy triviality about much of his banter that somehow warned everybody concerned not to take a lot of what he said too seriously. Also, since he did not allow direct quotation of his remarks, the news accounts of what he said did not carry quite the same documentary weight as direct quotation.

President Truman, however, was as blunt as a punch in the nose. He was pugnacious and cocky in answering reporters' questions, and during one of his tired periods he became involved in a spectacular press-conference controversy that still stands as a symbol of the dangers of imprecision in this question-and-answer game. It occurred in November of 1950, a particularly sensitive and even dangerous period because the Chinese Communists had just entered the Korean War as the American Army, advancing beyond the North-South dividing line of the 38th parallel, approached the Chinese border.

In preparation for the day's press conference, President Truman and his aides had held a series of private meetings to decide what the President's reaction should be. In the interests of precision, a careful statement was prepared which the President read to the reporters, but this merely expressed determination on the part of the United States government to remain steadfast in the face of the intervention of the Chinese Communists. One reporter, pressing for a more newsworthy lead, asked whether the atomic bomb might be used if necessary. The President replied that the use of the atomic bomb in emergencies was "always under consideration," whereupon the old technique of the punch lead and the flaming headline dropped the "always" and emphasized the "under consideration."

Some of the reporters in the room sensed the danger and, by follow-up questions, tried to give the President an opportunity to clarify the impression that he was actually considering use of the atomic bomb against the Chinese, as indeed he had in the previous war against the Japanese. One of my colleagues, Anthony Leviero of *The New York Times*, tried to underline the serious implications of the ambiguity by asking whether Mr. Truman would authorize direct quotation of his remarks on the subject. The President refused, and no effort was made to clarify his meaning until after the accounts of the conference were out in the world.

The news accounts of this sent a shudder through various capitals, and brought Prime Minister Clement Attlee flying to Washington for reassurance, but the damage was done. The record of this incident happens to be particularly complete because John Hersey, the novelist, was visiting at the White House during those days to do a long report on Mr. Truman for *The New Yorker* magazine. He testifies that at no time during the private meetings about the Chinese intervention in Korea was there ever any thought of using atomic weapons to deal with the Chinese menace. Yet the old political and journalistic techniques prevailed. Mr. Truman neither stuck to the precision of the written word nor fell back on Mr. Roosevelt's prudent refusal to answer what he called "iffy" questions; and at least some of the reporters persisted in the old habit of boring in for a better headline point, as if they were interviewing some heavyweight boxer on a forthcoming fight.

The incident, of course, magnifies and distorts the problem. Most of the time, Presidents manage to sense the moments of danger and evade particularly dangerous questions. After President Truman, Presidents Eisenhower and Kennedy increased the possibility of accident by permitting televised accounts of their news conferences, which have, in general, been useful without leading to any dramatic blunders. Yet there are times when provocative questions, once asked, cannot be evaded for political reasons, or answered without adding to tension between nations.

When King Faisal of Saudi Arabia came to the United States in June 1966, for example, he was asked by a reporter at the National Press Club in Washington to explain the Arab boycott of American concerns that trade with Israel. For political reasons he felt he had to answer that "we consider those who provide assistance to our enemies as our own enemies"; and, having answered as he did, the Governor of New York and the Mayor of New York City canceled their ceremonial occasions in his honor, thus spoiling the "good will" which was the purpose of his visit in the first place.

On and Off the Record

For a time after the last world war, officials and reporters, recognizing the dangers of these open press conferences, did devise one or two procedures for exchanging information in private. An organization called the Overseas Writers, composed of American reporters who had worked abroad and returned to Washington, would invite an official to address them at luncheon meetings on what was called a "background basis." This meant that the reporters could print the information, provided they did not identify the source. 1386279

However, as more and more American reporters served abroad, the organization became so large that officials began to feel that they could not talk freely without getting into trouble. One such incident occurred when General Omar Bradley, Chairman of the Joint Chiefs of Staff, said in answer to a question one day that, speaking as a soldier, he could see some advantages in rearming the Germans. Within an hour of that meeting some reporter present reported, and distorted, his remarks in a private conversation with an official of the French Embassy. By 5:30 of the same afternoon, a French official was at the State Department seeking assurance that the United States was against rearming the Germans, and within forty-eight hours General Bradley's views were being openly discussed and denounced in the French press. General Bradley's enthusiasm for further private meetings with Washington reporters was not pronounced.

Politics in the United States also create similar problems abroad, for what is "good politics" is not necessarily good diplomacy. Richard Nixon underscored the point in 1954 when he was Vice President and undertook to talk "off the record" to more than a thousand members of the American Society of Newspaper Editors in Washington. Talking off the record to a thousand people in the United States is like making love in Grand Central Station, but politically it was an effective performance, and maybe even a personal triumph.

Having just come back from Southeast Asia, Mr. Nixon said that the United States must send troops to Viet Nam, if necessary, to prevent a Communist victory in that country. He criticized the policies of the British and French governments, spoke critically of Syngman Rhee, then President of South Korea, and expressed the personal opinion that Robert Oppenheimer, then under investigation by the security board of the Atomic Energy Commission, was loyal but maybe a "security risk."

The editors had an informative luncheon, and before long, President Eisenhower, who was away playing golf in Augusta, Georgia, and Secretary of State Dulles, who was off at his cabin on an island in Lake Ontario, had a diplomatic incident to correct. Most reporters attributed Mr. Nixon's views to "a high Administration official," but within an hour it was all over Washington who the "high official" was. The correspondent of *The Times* of London, who was not present at the luncheon and therefore did not feel obliged to conceal the source, filed the whole story.

By the next day, Mr. Nixon's criticisms of President Rhee and the British and the French were published in the newspapers of those countries, the American people were being advised for the first time that some high officials thought the country might have to go to war in Viet Nam, and the Atomic Energy Commission's security board was being advised through the newspapers that Nixon had told a thousand editors that he thought Mr. Oppenheimer might be a "security risk."

Mr. Nixon certainly did not intend to cause all the commotion. He was doing naturally what would have been all right when the United States was an isolated country. He merely intended to make a good impression on a lot of editors who might help his political ambitions some day, and in the process stumbled into a foreign affairs tangle which embarrassed everybody concerned.

Thus each of these incidents tends to take on a life of its own and perpetuates the feeling abroad that American officials are too inexperienced to exercise safely the immense power they have over the lives of other peoples. If a President under probing questions, or a Vice President making hay with a lot of editors, gives an imprudent, silly, incomplete, or even misleading answer, this often has its effects overseas, and the politicians and editorial writers and commentators pick it up, only to be followed by official explanations and more criticisms of the explanations. This is the way it goes, often without personal intent on the part of either the questioner or the official, but the trouble ensues because old techniques are being used in a different time; and the consequences are not unimportant.

The Price of Criticism

In times of high controversy over policy, this constant thrust and counterthrust of public comment and criticism have a serious effect on officials. The more their policies are challenged, the more time they spend on defending their policies, until the words become as important as the acts, and the defense of policy takes on more meaning and consumes more time than the policy itself.

The energy devoted by the President and the Secretaries of State and Defense to the public-relations aspects of foreign policy now is almost beyond calculation. When they are being criticized, they seem all the more eager to argue their case in public. The President not only makes periodic addresses over the television networks, but usually makes himself available every day to repeat some statement for the national newscasters.

Not satisfied with the pressures generated in Washington, he calls in the governors, the mayors, the businessmen, and the press in an effort to get their support, or at least their understanding. Meanwhile, his Secretaries of State and Defense are constantly appearing before a Congress that refuses to modernize its procedures and forces cabinet members to appear before the separate foreign affairs and appropriations committees of both houses.

If we really knew the cost of all this physical and nervous strain on the principal officers of our government, we would probably be alarmed. The pressure merely of being agreeable to critics in the press and the Congress must by itself be a trial, and it certainly leaves little time for official reflection on anything except the particular crisis in the headlines at the moment. The Atlantic Alliance may be falling apart, but if the focus of the news is on the war in Viet Nam, that is what commands the attention of the press, the Congress and the public, that is what the questions are about, and therefore that is what the top officials are likely to be thinking about.

Nor have we devised effective remedies for putting things in perspective, despite all the battalions of official press officers and diplomatic press attachés now attached to the American government in Washington and abroad. At the State Department, the men who are available to most reporters are not informed on the details of the main news, and the men who are informed are so busy dealing with the current crisis that they have no time to be available.

The obvious conclusion to be drawn is that neither the press nor the government has kept pace with the torrent of change; and the surprising thing is not that this lag in attitudes and institutions is so great, but that under the circumstances the system works as well as it does.

Who is to say where the balance lies between the good aspects and the bad aspects of an aggressive and critical press? The system does serve as a check on reckless ventures, and at the same time it often limits negotiation and adds greatly to the personal strains on the officials concerned. Two distinguished historians have illustrated both sides of the dilemma.

Thomas A. Bailey, for example, provides one example against the press: "Journalistic ethics on the whole have been raised markedly in recent years, but there is still room for improvement. In 1942, the battle of Midway, which marked a turning point in the Pacific war, was won largely because our Navy 'cracked' the secret Japanese code. A large if not great Chicago newspaper later published information which indicated that this feat had been accomplished. The Japanese promptly changed their code, thereby making much more difficult our already hazardous operations in the Pacific. Even if we assume that the people are entitled to know everything, certainly the enemy is not."

And, on the other side, Arthur Schlesinger, Jr., commented thus on Secretary of State John Foster Dulles's relations with the press: "Washington newspapermen today hardly know whether to believe the Secretary of State, because they do not know if he is speaking to them as reporters or seeking to use them as instruments of psychological warfare. . . . What is the responsibility of a newspaperman when he discovers that some rumored development of policy is really only a psychological warfare trick? Should he print the truth at the risk of wrecking the plans of the Secretary of State? Or should he suppress the truth, betray himself, and deceive the American people?"

These are good questions, and they are even harder to answer than Schlesinger suggests, because the Secretary of State is always talking to various audiences at the same time. He may be talking mainly to the American people, but his words are also studied with the greatest care in Moscow and Peking. In this kind of world, where there are no longer merely "local" separate audiences for either officials or reporters, the problem is to try to find ways of bringing the old techniques up to date without crippling the function of a free but responsible press.

IV

THE PRESIDENT
AND THE PRESS

A Popular Fallacy

Nearly all American Presidents have arrived in office praising the press, and departed condemning many of its practices. Editors are very fond of quoting Thomas Jefferson's remark that he would not hesitate to choose "newspapers without a government" rather than the converse, but in the end he changed his mind. "The man who never looks into a newspaper is better informed than he who reads them," he concluded in a letter to John Norvell. This is not often quoted at journalistic conventions.

Modern Presidents have said much the same thing, only not so memorably. Woodrow Wilson started the first regular White House press conference by saying to the reporters: "I feel that a large part of the success of public affairs depends on the newspapermen—not so much on the editorial writers, because we can live down what they say, as upon the news writers, because the news is the atmosphere of public affairs." But before long he was saying to Senator Stone of Missouri: "I am so accustomed to having everything reported erroneously that I have almost come to the point of believing nothing that I see in the newspapers."

President Truman, pleading rather sadly with a columnist for self-censorship on military information, wrote: "I wish you'd do a little soul searching and see if at *great* intervals, the President may be right." According to Theodore Sorensen, President Kennedy never doubted the accuracy of Oscar Wilde's observation: "In America, the President reigns for four years, but Journalism governs forever."

This theme runs right through the testimony of the Presidents: they could do anything with public support, and nothing without it; and somehow an all-powerful and often irresponsible press made all the difference.

I once had a rather poignant experience with President Johnson that illustrates the point. This was in the summer of 1964 before the Democratic Party's Presidential nominating convention. Conversation in Washington at the time was on two main topics. A few days before, there had been a rather silly story in the press about the President driving his car at more than eighty miles an hour along a highway in Texas. Some accounts said the President had a paper cup of beer in the car, and after the headline writers got through with it, the impression given was of the President drinking and speeding. There was a lot of petty gabble about this in town, most of it exaggerated at the President's expense. The other topic was about the President's choice of a Vice Presidential candidate, and particularly whether his Attorney General, Robert Kennedy, brother and principal adviser to the assassinated President, was in the running for the job.

I went to the White House to get a line on this second topic and had a very long talk with the President alone. He spoke at great length about the Vice Presidency, and after about an hour, Jack Valenti, one of his aides, brought in the early edition of the week's *Time* magazine. The President got up from his rocking chair and went to his desk to read the account of the driving incident. When he came back, he was silent for a moment and obviously troubled.

Then he said that he wanted to do only one thing as President of the United States: "I want to unify this country." But he doubted whether he could do so because of the hostility of some elements in the press. There was in this country, he went on, a group of papers and writers determined to make him look like "an irresponsible hick." I tried to interrupt, but he wouldn't let me. He really wondered, he said sadly, whether we were "far enough away from Appomattox" for a Southern President to be able to unify the country. I was so disturbed by this that I finally managed to blurt out that he had problems with the press but nobody was trying to cut him up because he was a Southerner, and we had enough problems in the South without imagining things that weren't true. No, he concluded, it was true, and maybe we were talking about the wrong question. The question he had to decide was not whether Bobby Kennedy was in the running for the Vice Presidency, but whether he (the President) would agree to be nominated under the circumstances. I went away sad and astonished.

In the past, and in domestic affairs even now, it may be true that the influence of the press is so great; but in the field of foreign policy today, this concept of an all-powerful press seems to me to be out of date and wildly inaccurate.

I believe that the power of the Presidency has been increasing steadily since World War II, particularly since the introduction of nuclear weapons, and that the power of the press and even of the Congress to restrain the Chief Executive has declined proportionately during this same period.

Presidential power in the foreign field is in direct proportion to the size of the issue. The press can irritate and humiliate him personally. It can embarrass him by premature disclosure of his plans, and the Congress can still oppose and even defy him on peripheral issues. But on the great acts of foreign policy, especially those involving the risk or even the act of war, he is more powerful in this age than in any other, freer to follow his own bent than any other single political leader in the world—and the larger and more fateful the issue, the greater is his authority to follow his own will.

As the leader of a world-wide coalition of nations, engaged in constant contention with hostile forces in scores of different theaters of action or maneuver, he is virtually assured of support once he proclaims his intentions. The Congress, of course, retains its power to deny him the funds to carry out his plans, but it cannot do so without repudiating him in the face of the enemy and assuming responsibility for the crisis that would surely follow.

The Power of the White House

President Johnson's use of the so-called Congressional Resolution on Viet Nam illustrates this point. The Congress did not initiate that resolution. It was written in the State Department and sent to the Congress for approval on the morning after Communist PT boats made an unsuccessful attack on U.S. destroyers patrolling in the Gulf of Tonkin off North Viet Nam. It was not limited to the specific attack or even to the specific country at war. It asked the Congress to give the President authority to use whatever power "he" deemed necessary, not only in the Gulf of Tonkin or in Viet Nam but anywhere in all of Southeast Asia against any Communist aggression.

Obviously, the Congress complied, with very little debate and with only two dissenting votes. Once the request was made public and printed all over the world, the Congress could scarcely have done otherwise. The Congress followed the procedure initiated by President Eisenhower in the Formosan and Lebanon resolutions of the 1950s, and for similar situations in the future it is hard to imagine any Congress—even one dominated by the opposition party—doing otherwise.

The gravity of the issues since the advent of the cold war and atomic weapons has clearly enhanced the power of the President. In fact, I cannot think of a single major foreign policy move any President has wanted to make since World War II that he has been unable to carry through because of the opposition of the press or of the Congress.

President Truman ended World War II by ordering the use of atomic weapons on the Japanese. No political leader had ever used so much power with so little opposition. He launched the great recovery program for Europe, negotiated the most ambitious alliance in the history of the Atlantic nations, committed the nation to oppose Communist armed aggression anywhere in the world under the Truman Doctrine, and responded to war in Korea—all with very little opposition from the Congress or the press, and some of it without even asking the Congress.

President Wilson died believing that the balance of political power in America had swung so far toward the Senate that no President would ever be able to pass another major treaty. Yet President Eisenhower and his Secretary of State, John Foster

Dulles, scattered treaty commitments all over the Middle East and South Asia with scarcely a dissenting voice in the Congress or in the press. President Kennedy waged one proxy war against Cuba and risked a nuclear war with the Soviet Union over that same island without even asking the Congress. President Johnson sent more than 400,000 men to war in Viet Nam despite some sharp criticism from many of the nation's leading newspapers and commentators.

I do not say this is right or wrong, but merely that it is a fact of the nuclear age. In the Cuban missile crisis of 1962, President Kennedy was free to blockade Cuba, or bomb Havana, or, for that matter, as one of his advisers proposed at the time, to do nothing, on the excuse that since we had missiles in Turkey, why not permit Soviet missiles in Cuba? President Eisenhower was free to send his bombers to Dienbienphu in 1954 to relieve the French or to refuse to do so, just as he was free to go to the help of Hungary when it was invaded by the Red Army or to pass by on the other side. President Johnson was obviously free to bomb North Viet Nam or not to bomb it, to negotiate with Hanoi or to blow it up, to mine the harbor of Haiphong or to leave it alone. But in all cases the ultimate decision was up to the President.

Almost all scientific and political trends are enhancing the power of the President more than they are increasing the power of the Congress or the press. He alone has the authority, as Commander in Chief, to order the use of atomic weapons. He is charged with the security of the nation, which rests in large measure on his ability to persuade any hostile power that it cannot make a successful attack on America or America's major allies without risking self-destruction. This assurance rests on a single fact: aircraft and submarines equipped with hydrogen weapons are on patrol twenty-four hours a day in the air and under the oceans of the world, under the personal command of the President. No sovereign in history ever had such power or responsibility.

News and Opinion

The President's influence is increasing in other ways. Modern communications extend the reach and influence of reporters everywhere, but not so much as they expand the power of the President. The jet airplane has transformed diplomacy. On an hour's notice the President can decide that he wishes to be his own principal negotiator in a foreign land. Immediately, mobile radio transmitters, with all their modern contrivances for scrambling secret Presidential communications, are dispatched to the country concerned. The President's limousine, his teleprompters, even his special chair are loaded into flying boxcars and put down in a few hours in the capital concerned. We may report the news, but he makes it. If Senators are dominating the front pages with their protests against his foreign policy, and professors and editors are creating newsworthy disturbances on the university campuses and on the editorial pages, the President has a convenient remedy. He can divert public attention to himself. He can arrange a conference on an island in the Pacific, for example. Within seventy-two hours, he can bring the leaders of the nations on his side to a meeting that will arrest the interest of the world. Reporters and photographers will converge from all the capitals and fill the front pages with accounts of the proceedings, thereby overwhelming the less dramatic Senatorial mutterings.

This gives the President quite an edge. The reporters and commentators on the scene may see all this as an elaborate camouflage of realities and write their waspish critiques of the proceedings at his conference; but unless the great man is incorrigibly clumsy, which, with the help of an experienced Civil Service, he usually is not, the big front-page headlines will have much more effect than the witty chatter back on page 32.

In fact, the truth is that most American newspaper people are really more interested in dramatic spot news, the splashy story, than in anything else. They want to be in on the big blowout, no matter how silly, and would rather write about what happened than whether it made any sense.

The two Roosevelts were the Presidents who first understood the primacy of news over opinion. Teddy Roosevelt used to joke that he "discovered Monday." He recognized that editors had little news on Sunday night, and that if he held back his Presidential announcements until then, he got a better display on the front pages on Monday morning, even with secondary news, than he got on Wednesday with really important news. Later, President Taft observed in a letter to Elihu Root, "Theodore is not the only pebble on the beach in the use of the press." The Wilson Administration, he wrote, was "masterly" in its use of the Washington correspondents: "It shows a keenness of the use of political instruments and an ability in this direction that rouses my very great admiration."

Franklin Roosevelt, who was elected to the Presidency four times against the overwhelming opposition of the American newspapers, was even better at dominating the news. He concentrated on the reporters and the front pages and vilified or scorned the commentators and the editorial pages.

No President has understood this technique better than Lyndon Johnson. He spent more than thirty years on Capitol Hill and remembers well that Presidents usually got in trouble when they did not retain the news initiative in the White House and allowed the Congress to dominate the headlines. Accordingly, he has constantly remained on top of the news with a ceaseless torrent of activity, speeches, meetings, trips, and messages to the Congress and leaders of the world.

Europe has a press that stresses opinion; America a press, radio, and television that emphasize news. The Lippmanns, the Krocks, the Alsops, and the brilliant young American satirists, Russell Baker of *The New York Times* and Art Buchwald, tickle the intellectuals and often come nearer to the truth than all the solemn analysts; but news is more powerful than opinion, a point that the politicians have understood. No doubt the commentators have considerable influence on the intellectual, political, and diplomatic communities, but in a big continental democratic country this is no majority. Even among the reporters of America, opinion is a secondary thing, and "pundit" is almost a term of derision. It is the man who comes first with the news of what the powerful American government is about to do who commands the most attention within his profession, and it is the television reporters who report the news to vast national audiences every day— Walter Cronkite, Chet Huntley and David Brinkley—who influence the mass.

In short, the President almost always has the initiative over both the press and the Congress if he chooses to use the instruments at his command. He is no "equal" partner with the Congress in the conduct of foreign affairs, if he ever was. He and he alone is in constant communication with almost every other leader in the world. He can reach his own countrymen from his television studio in the White House whenever great events justify a request for network time. It is now common practice for the President to devote part of many working days to repeating statements for the television cameras, so that he is in constant touch with the people.

As principal spokesman of the nation, the President tends to identify himself with its noblest ideals. The Chief Executive is able with a good show of reason to have the nation's ministers and publicists with him on "peace," the nation's professors and moral-izers with him on desegregation, the nation's economists with him on fiscal policy, and the nation's political scientists with him on civil rights and political reform. Thus, when the Congress is squabbling in the wings over Rule 22 or the intricacies of repeal-ing Section 14-b of the Taft-Hartley Act, the President is con-stantly proclaiming the brotherhood of man, progress, generosity toward the weak, and the elevation of the poor and under-developed.

Senators and Representatives, of course, appear on special question-and-answer programs, and they can and do question the President's foreign-policy actions on the floor of Congress; but a President speaking to twenty million people and a Senator ad-dressing half a dozen of his colleagues and empty galleries are not exactly the same thing. Until this time we have never had a President who had the opportunity, the will, and the ability to exploit television to the full. Franklin Roosevelt undoubtedly had the will and the ability, but he did not have access to national television networks. President Eisenhower had the opportunity, but not the will, to use them. President Kennedy had the ability but was afraid of appearing too often on the screen. And President Johnson has the will, though perhaps not the manner, to captivate a national audience. Some day we may very well have a President with the looks, the voice, and the charisma to unbalance the system even more than it is unbalanced now; but for the present, nobody need worry much about the press overwhelming a President who has all the miracles of modern electronics and transportation at his disposal.

The Presidential Press Conference

There is a theory, widely advertised at annual meetings of editors and publishers, that the modern Presidential press conference is a restraining influence on the Chief Executive. According to this notion, the reporters are representatives of the people, like members of the British House of Commons, who have the power to make the great man answer questions, usually about his shortcomings or failures. There is a shred of truth in this, but not much more.

President Johnson demonstrated his command of the press conference in a very simple way. He knew that the Washington press corps was full of specialists, some of whom had devoted most of their careers to the study of foreign affairs, or the Federal judiciary, or science, or military affairs, and therefore not only knew their subjects but probably knew more about them than he did. If he announced his news conferences in advance, they would come running with their well-informed and awkward inquiries. So he simply did not announce most of his news conferences in advance. He called them often when only the White House correspondents were around, and then usually on the weekends when only a few of them were on duty. He held them in his own executive office, where he was not on display before the cameras, but talking intimately on a first-name basis with the reporters who travel with him all the time and are not only familiar to him but subject to his system of punishments and rewards, which can be embarrassing to a reporter on a highly competitive beat.

The point here is not that this is wicked but merely that nobody need grieve too mournfully over the fiction of a poor, defenseless President badgered by a pack of insensitive and irresponsible barbarians. There is nothing in the Constitution that obliges him to conduct his office for the convenience of reporters. If he is experienced enough to get to the White House, he is usually nimble enough to handle the reporters who work there.

He knows the cast of characters. He decides whom to recognize and whom to ignore. He can always retreat into "No comment" or turn a troublesome question into a lecture on something else. Reporters, no matter how long on the White House beat, are not so different from other Americans. They are sentimental about the White House and respectful of the Presidency even if they happen to be critical of the incumbent of the day, and it is a rare journalistic lion who would dare react to an evasive Presidential answer with a request for a more responsive and detailed explanation.

Every President develops his own defenses in this situation. President Roosevelt scorned and ridiculed his questioners. He once awarded a Nazi Iron Cross to John O'Donnell of the *New York News* during World War II and ordered Robert Post of *The New York Times* to put on a dunce cap and stand in the corner. Asking President Truman a question was like pitching batting practice to the Yankees. He decapitated you and then grinned. President Eisenhower was amiably incomprehensible. President Kennedy, the real master of "the game," was a witty computer. He either overwhelmed you with decimal points or disarmed you with a smile and a wisecrack. And President Johnson learned early to apply to the press conference the technique of the Senate filibuster.

From the start of his Administration, President Johnson regarded the press conference not primarily as a duty to respond to questions about his stewardship but as an opportunity to put over his views—an old FDR device—and he quickly learned that the more he talked, the less time there was for questions. Accordingly, a good part of his carefully timed conferences are taken up with executive announcements which in other Administrations would probably have been put out by the White House Press Secretary, and when the occasion finally gets around to questions, his answers are often long soliloquies, many of them interesting and some of them even relevant.

Few creatures are more tiresome than whining reporters, and I don't want to fall into this occupational hazard of tedious self-pitying. But some things are changing in these power relations around the White House that may be of importance not primarily to reporters but to readers and viewers and citizens.

President Johnson's News Techniques

President Johnson thinks of reporters in subjective rather than in objective terms, as individuals rather than as instruments of a free press in a free society. He knows all about the theory of the press conference as a means of raising questions that may be on the people's mind, and he defends the theory as a theory but not as a regular practice. Franklin Roosevelt held news conferences twice a week before the 1939-45 war and once a week when we were in that war. President Kennedy held formal news conferences, announced in advance, about once every two weeks. President Johnson held only nine formal advance-notice news conferences in 1965.

This, however, distorts the record and does not clarify his method. No President in the history of the Republic has ever devoted so much time to reporters, editors, and commentators. But he sees them individually and at such length that the reporters themselves are often embarrassed to intrude so much on his other duties. It was not unusual last year for the President to sit casually in his rocking chair talking steadily to a reporter for a couple of hours, and sometimes even much longer than that.

This, of course, can be very helpful to the reporter concerned, but conversations of this length somehow imply, even if the President does not intend them to do so, a confidential, personal relationship that actually ties the reporter up more than it frees him to do his job. It is very difficult to sit and listen to a President explaining his terrible problems and narrow options without becoming sympathetic to the man and subjective about his policies. It is all the harder to remain detached about the range of topics discussed when he asks you what you would do in his place.

I do not say the system was adopted to achieve this close involvement. It is simply Lyndon Johnson's way of doing things. When he was Majority Leader of the Senate, *The New York Times*'s reporter on that beat was William S. White, a Texan whom he liked and admired. When White resigned from *The Times*, I assigned Russell Baker to cover the Senate, and when Baker got bored with it several months later, I asked Ned Kenworthy to take on the job. At this point, Mr. Johnson took me aside and asked what was going on. He had to know who was covering him, he said. He couldn't have one fellow one day and another the next. I tried to explain, but it was no use. He simply thought of the job in personal terms, and he has retained this attitude in the White House, despite the efforts of his Press Secretaries to persuade him it wouldn't work.

The power of the President to use the free press against itself is also very great. If, for example, an influential columnist or commentator criticizes him for landing 25,000 Marines in the Dominican Republic to put down a rebellion, it is very easy for him to call in several other carefully selected commentators and give them the detailed argument for landing the Marines. He has all the vivid facts of the situation, and if he wants to put them out, he does not have to announce them himself. Other reporters will be perfectly willing to accommodate him, even though they know they are being used to knock down the story of a colleague.

The function of criticism itself has changed in an odd way during President Johnson's Administration. In the past, there was a reasonable expectation among people writing political criticism that if they identified a problem, checked it out thoroughly, and proposed a reasonable remedy, publication of these things would be read within the government in good faith and maybe even considered worthy of executive action.

This is still true today on questions of policy, but if the topic deals with individuals in the Administration, the chances are that the criticism will perpetuate the situation criticized. For example, if you write today that a particular cabinet member has been exhausted by overwork and should be liberated for his own and the nation's good, you can be fairly sure that you have condemned that man to stay at his grindstone until everybody has forgotten that you ever mentioned him.

Also, if you learn that the President is going to do something on Friday and print it on Tuesday, this effort in journalistic enterprise is likely to be regarded as an impertinence and a presumption which the President will punish by changing his plans. I once saw the speech President Johnson was going to make at the twentieth anniversary celebration of the founding of the United Nations and printed his thoughts on ending the financial crisis that was going on in the U.N. at that time. He was furious. He called in the Secretary of State the same night of publication, ordered the speech rewritten to eliminate the reported plans, and made a different speech.

This privilege is fair enough, but behind it there is a philosophic idea that has some disturbing possibilities. Bill Moyers, as White House Press Secretary, explained the President's view in these terms: "It is very important for a President to maintain up until the moment of decision his options, and for someone to speculate days or weeks in advance that he's going to do thus and thus is to deny to the President the latitude he needs in order to make, in the light of existing circumstances, the best possible decision."

No doubt such latitude is necessary in many circumstances, but not in all. Is absolutely nothing to be printed about clandestine plans by the President to mount an illegal invasion at the Bay of Pigs in Cuba, for fear of interfering with the President's option to humiliate the country? Are the people to be denied information about Presidential options that will involve them in a war they have to finance and fight? If all Presidential options are to be protected from speculation "until the very last minute," what redress will there be the day after the President has opted to dispatch the Marines, or bomb Hanoi, or publish a request to wage war all over Southeast Asia as "he" deems necessary?

These are hard questions, and the answers are not that the Commander in Chief must telegraph all his punches in advance. But at the same time, the doctrine of no-speculation-before-official-publication, even on nonmilitary matters, is something new in the catalogue of Presidential privilege.

Criticism and Patriotism

Presidential privilege does not extend to the point of abolishing dissent or suggesting that somehow dissenters are unpatriotic. The chances are that the United States is going to be engaged for the rest of the century in political crises and limited wars in some part of the world, most of them under highly ambiguous circumstances where there will usually be room for doubt about what is the best course of action. These crises will always bear most heavily on the President. The enemy will always use criticism in the American press against him; and the President will always be tempted, while defending the principle of dissent, to protest that the dissent is hampering his conduct of the war and hurting the country.

In the so-called Philippine Insurrection of 1899-1902, with 60,000 American troops fighting Asian rebels, President McKinley made a speech in Pittsburgh calling American opponents of that war "unpatriotic"—and there were plenty of opponents then, too. According to Secretary of the Treasury Lyman Gage who was present, the McKinley cabinet spent most of one entire session debating whether the *Springfield Republican,* the *Boston Herald,* the *New York Evening Post,* and *The Nation* should be prosecuted for treason.

President Johnson did not go this far in the Viet Nam war. Yet nobody was more eloquent in defense of the principle of dissent, or more resentful of its practice in that particular conflict. "Put away all the childish divisive things," he argued, "if you want the maturity and the unity that is the mortar of a nation's greatness. I do not think that those men who are out there fighting for us tonight think we should enjoy the luxury of fighting each other back home. . . . The road ahead is going to be difficult. There will be some nervous Nellies and some who will become frustrated and bothered and break ranks under the strain and turn on their own leaders, their own country, and their own fighting men."

And again from President Johnson: "If you are too busy or not inclined to help, please count ten before you hurt. Because we must have no doubt today about the determination of the American men wearing American uniforms, the Marines who are out there fighting in the wet jungles, wading through the rice paddies up to their belts, the sailors who are searching the shores and patrolling the seas, the airmen who are out there facing the missiles and antiaircraft guns, carrying out their missions, trying to protect your liberty. These men are not going to fail us. Now the real question is: Are we going to fail them? Our staying power is what counts in the long and dangerous months ahead. The Communists expect us to lose heart. . . . They believe that the political disagreements in Washington, the confusion and doubt in the United States, will hand them a victory on a silver platter in Southeast Asia."

This is a powerful and troubling argument, for criticism does raise problems. In the Vietnamese war, what the President said was true about the assumptions of the enemy, but it raises some fundamental questions. For the White House argument was, first, that there can be no speculation before official publication about what the President's course of action will be, and, second, that after he decides to make war, the only patriotic thing to do is to support the President in defense of the "vital interests" of the country. In short, no speculation before war and no criticism after. This is an interesting thesis, especially since Senator Lyndon Johnson himself argued in 1954 that the United States should not intervene in Viét Nam because it was not "vital" to the security of the United States.

As Walter Lippmann wrote in 1965, "If the President's version of history is correct, it follows that when there is an issue of war and peace, the only safe and patriotic course is to suspend debate and rally around the President. . . . It amounts to saying that debate on the vital issues of war and peace gives aid and comfort to the enemy. Under such a rule, the American people would have had no right to debate the momentous question of whether in 1917 and 1939 they should emerge from the isolationism which they had practiced since Washington's Farewell Address and the Declaration of the Monroe Doctrine. This is an impossible course for a free people. . . . How else but by debate are the great questions of war and peace—of isolation and intervention and of military expansion onto the Asian continent—to be decided?"

Lippmann argues that it is a fallacy to consider that a divided public opinion in the United States will have any effect on the enemy. I do not agree. The essence of the problem is that there is a great deal to be said for both the dangers and the necessity of criticism. The testimony of George Reedy, who served as President Johnson's White House Press Secretary, probably comes nearer the truth of the dilemma. After he left the White House, still a close friend and devoted supporter of the President, he nevertheless came to an interesting conclusion about the natural differences between the role of the newspaperman and that of the statesman.

"A political leader," Reedy observed, "is essentially an advocate—a man who is seeking to shape the world toward ends he considers worthy. . . . A newspaperman, on the other hand, is one whose job is to chronicle daily events and to place the facts before the public in some reasonable perspective. Events and facts have a life of their own. They are independent of the dreams and desires of men. . . . On that basis, it is obvious that there must be a divergency of viewpoints between the political leader, who assesses public communications in terms of help or hindrance toward a worthy goal; and the newspaperman, who assesses public communications in terms of their consonance with what he regards as reality—however harsh. . . . A democratic society is inconceivable without tension, and the objective reporting that democracy requires will always produce tension. I might add that I do not think that our country has ever been hurt by skeptical and rambunctious newspapermen."

No doubt this is hard on the President. As Reedy observes, it adds an additional burden on the leaders who are the focus of tensions even when the press is contented, serene, and harmonious. The President is the principal actor on the stage. He has to take responsibility for his actions, and the press does not. Therefore, he tries constantly to use whatever devices he can to ease the agony. He manages the news, as the heads of all institutions do, by emphasizing his successes and minimizing his losses. He has his own photographers constantly taking his picture and releases those that convey the impression of strong leadership or compassion or whatever other mood he wants to convey at the moment. All this is understandable, but we should not be fooled: the trend of power is running with the President, the major danger of excessive use of power lies not in the newspapers but in the White House, and even the most casual look at the influence of reporters and commentators today makes this fairly obvious.

V

THE INFLUENCE
OF THE PRESS

As Ally of the Government

THE INFLUENCE of the American press on American foreign policy, in my view, is usually exaggerated. Its influence is exercised primarily through the Congress, which confuses press opinion with public opinion; through foreign embassies and the foreign press in Washington, which think we know more about what is going on in the Federal capital than we really do; and through the universities of America, which, ironically, have a kind of intellectual contempt for the press, but read it more avidly, more critically, and probably more accurately than we read it ourselves. No doubt, the press has great influence on American foreign policy when things are *obviously* going badly; it has very little influence, however, when things are going badly but the impending disaster is not obvious and the government is saying, as it usually does, that all is well or soon will be if everybody only has faith and confidence.

Newspapers, radio, and television stations in the United States influence foreign policy mainly by reporting the actions of government. Acts are more powerful than words in this field and news more influential than opinion. Most of the time, reporters are in the distributing business, transmitting the accounts of what Presidents and Secretaries of State do onto the front pages and into the top headlines, where they undoubtedly influence public opinion. Let me make the news, Franklin Roosevelt said in effect, and you can write all the editorials you like against it.

Most of the time, contrary to official mythology, the people who write the news are not the enemies but the allies of officials. They are usually delivering the news as the post office delivers the mail, and when officials and reporters perform this cooperative service, which is what they do most of the time, they are undoubtedly an influential combination.

I remember writing the first detailed story about the government's vague thoughts for a European Recovery Plan in the spring of 1945. It appeared in column one of page one of a Sunday edition of *The New York Times*, leading with the news that the Truman Administration was considering a five-year plan that would cost about $20 billion. Before nine o'clock that Sunday morning, Senator Arthur Vandenberg of Michigan, then Chairman of the Senate Foreign Relations Committee, telephoned me at home. "Either you are wrong," he said, "or this government is out of its mind. Any plan of that size is out of the question."

Yet after a few months of official speeches and explanations, of transatlantic meetings and conferences on Capitol Hill, all of them making front-page news, public support for the plan developed and Vandenberg, with some sympathetic and convivial guidance from Dean Acheson, led the fight to get it through the Senate.

Secretary of State George C. Marshall, who launched the plan that later bore his name, conceded when it was all over that the support of the newspapers and commentators had contributed greatly to its success. "I found, as in almost everything I touched," he said, "it is not so hard to make a general plan; the great problem is how to put that thing over, how you carry it through, and that was the case in this instance."

Much depends, of course, on who makes the news. Senator J. W. Fulbright, one of Vandenberg's successors as Chairman of the Foreign Relations Committee, commanded the news in the spring of 1966 by staging a series of nationally televised hearings that were critical of the Johnson Administration's policy toward Viet Nam and China. The hearings also had some influence on foreign policy for a time, not for but against the Administration's line; however, it is the executive and not the legislative branch of the Federal government that usually dominates the headlines.

Washington reporters also assist the government and influence foreign policy in more oblique ways. For example—though officials seldom like to talk about this—reporters are constantly used to transmit to foreign governments, through press, radio, and television, those official views which the Administration in Washington does not want to put in formal diplomatic communications. One reason for this is that the old diplomacy, with its polite but geometric language, has broken down, and the new diplomacy— part secret, part public, part propaganda—has devised new techniques of communication between governments and peoples.

The notion that the mass of the people of a nation should become deeply involved in foreign-policy questions was regarded in the nineteenth century as preposterous, if not downright reckless. George Canning was probably the first statesman who recognized what he called the "fatal artillery of popular excitation," and Prince Metternich was appalled. He accused Canning of seeking "popularity—a pretension that is misplaced in a statesman."

In fact, the diplomats of the old school were so cautious about arousing popular emotion over foreign-policy questions that they invented a whole catalogue of technical phrases or guarded understatements that enabled them to say harsh things to one another without being impolite or provoking public concern. Thus Harold Nicolson reminds us that Wellington once referred to a bloody massacre as "the transactions complained of." Thus, too, if the British Foreign Office requested, with exquisite politeness, a reply to a note by "six in the evening of September 5," this was recognized in every foreign office in the world, but usually not by the people, as an ultimatum threatening forthwith a military response to the controversy.

All this tidy discretion was overwhelmed by the propaganda of the two world wars and the blunter undiplomatic language of Moscow and Washington in the 1940s. Nevertheless, the problem of transmitting guarded warnings from one government to another remains, and it is the reporters who are very often used to perform this function in the United States today.

When, for example, the French government indicated in 1966

that it intended to withdraw its military forces from the integrated command of the North Atlantic Treaty Organization and force all NATO troops to accept French control or get out of France, the American government, hoping to forestall the move without threatening the French, "inspired" certain news stories through American reporters on the unpleasant consequences of such action by France. The meaning of these news dispatches was perfectly clear to the French government, though they did not bring about a change in French policy.

To cite another example: for over two years, during most of the Kennedy and the first part of the Johnson Administrations, the United States government supported in the North Atlantic Treaty Organization the idea of an international surface fleet armed with nuclear weapons. The crews would be made up of men from various Allied nations but subject to American control over the actual firing of nuclear weapons. This was bitterly opposed by the Soviet Union on the ground that it gave the NATO Allies, including the Germans, "access" to nuclear information and experience. It was also opposed by some members of the Alliance on the ground that it would weaken their national authority without actually giving them equality in an international force.

The opposition from both Moscow and some of the Allies became so strong after President Johnson came to power that he decided to shelve the whole idea in order to reassure the new governments of Harold Wilson in London and of Kosygin and Brezhnev in Moscow. Since he did not, however, wish to repudiate formally the position he and President Kennedy had taken in the past, he told a reporter of his plans and allowed him to publish the decision, which was not even known to his own ambassadors in Moscow or the NATO countries at the time of publication. Later, and privately, the report in *The New York Times* was confirmed to governments that requested an explanation. This illustrates one of the official-reporter diplomatic techniques of modern diplomacy, and also demonstrates one of the scientific oddities of the age, namely, that a government is the only known vessel that leaks from the top.

As Critic of the Government

The influence of press, radio, and television when they act against the foreign policy of a government, however, is not so powerful as when they are transmitting the government's views and commenting favorably upon them. Occasionally, one or two correspondents may uncover facts that are either unknown to or ignored by the government and, by publishing them, influence the government to investigate the published facts and adjust policy to meet them.

This happened from time to time during the Viet Nam war. For example, when the press reported the careless use of artillery fire and air power in South Viet Nam, leading to unnecessary civilian casualties, the government in Washington issued orders to minimize the element of accident. However, when news reports gave a much more pessimistic account of that war during most of 1963 and 1964 than the government itself was giving, the more optimistic claims of the top officials of the government were believed by most people until both the political and military situations began to collapse.

Much of the time, the influence of the press on foreign policy depends on the attitude of the President toward the press. President Eisenhower was irritated by the press and did not read it carefully. President Kennedy had his troubles with the press and once barred the *New York Herald Tribune* from the White House, but he read the newspapers avidly as a check against the activities of his own government. It was not unusual for him to call his Secretary of State or even one of the regional Assistant Secretaries before eight in the morning to ask for a report on some news account back on page 16 of *The New York Times*. Such attention greatly enhanced the influence of the press during his thousand days in the White House.

The President's attitude toward the press sets the pattern for the rest of his Administration. If he reads the newspapers carefully, his aides will read them to be prepared for that early morn-

ing call from the White House. If he likes, trusts, and sees reporters officially and socially, as President Kennedy did, then
cabinet members, Foreign Service officers, ambassadors and top
civil servants will tend to do the same. This is vital to a free press,
for a great deal of the most important news is gathered not from
the top of the government but from the experts on various
subjects and regions who "brief" the President and the others at
the top.

If, on the other hand, the President is known to be hostile to
the press or to certain of its leading commentators, he does not
have to tell his aides to be wary or to avoid what he regards as
his "enemies" in the press. They simply feel it is prudent in their
own self-interest to be "in conference" when reporters call or to
be extremely cautious and uncommunicative if they do see reporters.

An atmosphere of caution and reserve gradually came to influence the Johnson Administration, for example. The President
watched the press even more closely than his predecessor did, but
regarded it mainly as a problem rather than as an opportunity.
He had the Associated Press and United Press International news
tickers in a small cubbyhole off his main office and followed their
news files constantly throughout the day. He also installed not one
but three television sets both in his office and in his bedroom so
that he could watch all three national television networks at once.
During the noon and four o'clock news briefings by his White
House Press Secretary, Mr. Johnson would occasionally telephone
to give his own answer to some question posed a minute before by
a reporter, leading the press to the not very remarkable suspicion
that the President was listening in on the conference from another
room.

One wonders whether President Johnson consciously adopted
these habits to dominate the press and to keep his own aides
under control. Maybe so, maybe no. Probably he was mainly determined to keep in touch with everything that was going on.
Often, he would see an item on the ticker about some citizen in
trouble, or even some reporter in an accident, and out of kindness

would immediately telephone the family to express his sympathy and to offer his help. He did this once for me when I crashed in a naval airplane in Danang during the Viet Nam war, though his personal enthusiasm for my writings at that or any other time was not unbounded. Yet one effect of his preoccupations with the press and his savage and often cruel comments about members of the press corps to his associates was to curb the flow of the news, perhaps even more than he intended it to do.

Public criticism of government policy can, of course, influence policy, but it tends to do so not through persuading a mass audience but by reaching a much smaller audience in the Congress and the intellectual and communications communities of the nation. The editorial pages of American newspapers still reach a very limited percentage of the newspaper-reading public and, like the television commentators, tend to be dominated by the flow of news coming mainly from official sources.

Never have reporters and commentators reached so many people in America with their news and views as they do now, and had so little power to change the direction of the nation's foreign policy. The television network "stars" reach as many as 26 million viewers a night with their news summaries. They bring in their vivid reports on video tape from all the major capitals and battlefields of the world, and occasionally even bounce them off man-made stars in transoceanic broadcasts, but the reaction of the public in the foreign field is quite different from that in the national field.

Within the nation, reporters have a powerful influence on local and national issues. The local editor is usually a respected leader on community issues. The television reports of racial strife in the American South undoubtedly aroused the conscience of millions of viewers and helped produce the nationwide protest movements and the legislation that transformed the legal position of the American Negro in the mid-1960s.

In certain situations overseas, modern news reporting arouses Congressional and public opinion sufficiently to influence the President and his aides. News reports and television films of

American and South Vietnamese casualties undoubtedly helped encourage resistance to that war. Yet despite the enlarged scope and volume of reports to the American people from abroad, the President has seldom if ever been more free to conduct foreign policy in accordance with his own judgments, and the reasons for this are fairly clear.

The issues of foreign policy are increasingly complex and dangerous. It was easy to have a strong public opinion against getting involved in wars when the mood and tradition of the nation were powerfully isolationist, and easier still to get almost unanimous public support when wars started with an attack on Pearl Harbor or with the movement of enemy armies across recognized international frontiers. Even experts on foreign affairs, however, find it difficult to have dogmatic opinions about what to do when the nation is confronted with wars 10,000 miles from home started by subversion and guerrilla action under ambiguous circumstances carefully calculated by the enemy to confuse and deceive.

A fundamental change has thus occurred in the attitude of the American people toward the government's conduct of foreign policy. In the old days, the people tended to believe the government was wrong until war was actually declared; now, confronted with torrents of confusing and often contradictory information about questions that could lead to war, the tendency is to assume the government is right. I believe the American reporters were nearer to the truth than the published government reports were during the critical periods that preceded the indirect American invasion of Cuba in 1961 and the large American intervention in South Viet Nam in 1965, but the people paid little attention to those reports and the government was free to use its own judgment, which was not brilliant.

It takes some thumping crisis to startle a vast continental nation out of its normal preoccupations with family and work. There is a time problem here that minimizes the influence of newspapers on the public. To be effective, reports on a developing situation have to come considerably ahead of the crisis; but at that time the people are usually not paying attention, and once the crisis breaks, they tend to leave it to the government.

Besides, it is hard for even the most careful reader or listener or viewer to be sure when the reporters are right and when they are wrong, since we reporters are wrong so often. If we tell the readers a mayor is a crook and provide some evidence in support of the claim, they will usually believe us, but if we suggest the Secretary of State is a numskull or the President is a pleasant incompetent, they will usually tell us to mind our manners. Our power is smaller than our reputation. The credit of the American newspapers with the American people for accuracy and good judgment is not high. Everybody knows how often the American voters reject the advice of newspapers in local, state, and national elections: one word from us and they do as they please. And especially in the field of foreign policy, a majority of the people will usually take the government's judgment over that of the newspapers.

The Press and Congress

What influence the press has on the conduct of foreign policy usually comes indirectly, not through the mass of the people but mainly through the Congress of the United States. The relations between well-informed reporters in Washington and influential Congressmen are quite different from the relations between reporters and officials of the executive branch of the government.

Officials in the White House, the State Department, and the Defense Department, though polite and often friendly, almost always regard the reporter with suspicion. He is potential trouble. Even if the official tells the reporter nothing and puts it off the record as well, which often happens, the mere fact that he is known to have seen the reporter may lead his superiors to blame him for something the reporter prints several days later. Thus, the official is canny, particularly if the President or the Secretary of State happens to be in a waspish mood toward the press, which is the case a good deal of the time.

Congressmen are different. Unlike officials of the executive branch, they live most of the time in the open. They think the good opinion of the press is important to their re-election, which dominates much of their thinking; consequently, they see reporters and some of them even read us. Also, they are always making speeches and, like reporters, looking for mistakes to correct or criticize, especially if they are in the opposition.

Reporters and Congressmen are thus often natural allies. They exchange information in a discreet way, and sometimes in ways that are not so discreet. When the Administration comes to the Congressmen for its money, it has to answer their questions and justify its programs, and in the process it discloses a lot of information which interests the press a great deal. Particularly in these days when so much of foreign policy depends on economic and military appropriations that the Congress must approve, the committee hearings are often a profitable source of news.

How the press, radio, and television reporters use the close association with members of the Congress determines whether their influence is good or bad. Out of the hundreds of thousands of words spoken on a busy day in the committees and on the floor of the two houses of Congress, the reporters must make a selection, and what they select goes not only to all the newspapers and radio and television stations but also over those tickers outside the President's office. Thus the reporters at the White House are constantly conveying the views of the President to the members of the Federal legislature, and the reporters in the House and Senate press galleries are similarly serving as a link between what is happening on Capitol Hill and the President and his cabinet members, who also have news tickers in their offices.

What makes news in a democratic society thus influences policy decisions both in the executive and legislative branches of the government. The politicians at both ends of Pennsylvania Avenue are particularly sensitive to what the reporters select, what is going out on the air and into the headlines, for this often produces strong reactions among the voters outside Washington. In the battle for the appropriation of money, for example, the dramatic news of military requirements tends to get a larger play than the less spectacular news about foreign aid, and this news emphasis on the military undoubtedly helps assure more votes for the armed services than for the foreign aid programs.

The influence of reporters on the conduct of individual members of the House and Senate, particularly the House, is much greater than is generally realized. For example, if reporters tend to play up the spectacular charges or statements of extremists on Capitol Hill and to play down or ignore the careful, analytical speeches of the more moderate and responsible members—as, unfortunately, they do most of the time—this inevitably has its influence on many other members, particularly new members. The latter are naturally trying to establish themselves. They are eager to say things that will get into the news and be read back home before the next election. Accordingly, if the moderate and the serious statements are ignored by the reporters and the spectacular trivialities are emphasized, the new Congressman often draws the obvious conclusion and begins spouting nonsense to attract attention. This is one influence of a popular press in a democracy that merits more attention than it gets.

The Press and the Embassies

There is also a natural alliance between reporters and foreign diplomats in Washington, as there is between reporters and legislators. Each major embassy is staffed with experts who follow a particular subject or region of the world. They may be specialists on Asia or science or military affairs or agriculture, and they follow the entire range of American foreign policy, since it usually affects the interests of their own countries. Reporters in Washington gather a great deal of information from these men, and when it appears in the press, Congressmen often want to question cabinet members about it and can do so much more easily than the reporters who published it in the first place.

The relationship between reporters and diplomats is not only widely misunderstood but also underrated. Even well-informed and sophisticated Americans are often irritated by the toplofty pronouncements of American commentators, who seem to pass judgment on the Buddhists and Catholics in Viet Nam one day, explain the mysteries of Southern Rhodesia, the Congo, and South Africa the next, psychoanalyze Senator Fulbright and the Secretary of State on the third, and so on triumphantly through the week, without ever a doubt or a day of rest. It seems an impossibility and a presumption for any one man to know so much about so many things, but that is not the way it is.

Most of us are merely reporters of other men's ideas. Diplomats and reporters have one job in common: they have to report what is going on, the diplomat to his government, the reporter to his paper or station. All the influential people in Washington may be furious about France, but they will be polite to the French Ambassador. They will tell a thoughtful reporter what they really think about President de Gaulle's policy, though they will probably pull their punches when talking to de Gaulle's representative. Knowing this, the French Ambassador will often talk to a well-informed reporter. He will exchange information, but on one condition: the source of the information must not be disclosed.

Therefore, if the reporter is passing on information gathered by the French in Saigon or by the Canadian member of the International Control Commission on Viet Nam, he cannot disclose where he got the information. He must pretend that somehow, in his infinite knowledge and wisdom, this is the way things are, for to protect his sources, he is obliged to indulge in what we call "compulsory plagiarism."

In the process a great deal of useful information and political analysis is gathered. The diplomats are the unpaid stringers for the reporters, the reporters the unpaid tipsters for the diplomats. Ideas that professional diplomats might hesitate to mention to the Secretary of State, and information and analysis which the reporter probably would not have gathered in any other way, thus get into the newspapers and may sometimes even be read by the President—which may have been what the diplomat had in mind in the first place.

There is, too, a kind of international fraternity of reporters, as there is of scientists, and this also has some influence on American foreign policy. With the rise of American power in the world, the major newspapers and radio and television networks abroad send to Washington some of the most distinguished journalists in the world. Usually even the great newspapers like *The Times* of London or the *Manchester Guardian* or the *Neue Zürcher Zeitung* of Switzerland have only one or two reporters covering the entire range of American affairs. Therefore, they cooperate with one another, exchange information with the leading diplomatic correspondents of American papers and agencies, and often reflect the reports and comments of American papers in their own countries. The White House and the State Department cannot ignore the reports of these men. They have considerable influence not only on the intellectuals of their own countries but on their foreign offices as well, and what they gather on their own or through their associates on the American papers sooner or later is likely to raise questions at the top of the American government.

In such ways, American reporters and commentators no doubt do have influence. They keep the debate on foreign affairs going. They influence other editors who pass on their views and reports. They influence legislators not only by what they write but sometimes by what they say. For example, the Senate hearings on Viet Nam and China in 1966 probably would never have been held but for the suggestion of a reporter in Washington to the Chairman of the Senate Foreign Relations Committee.

To suggest, however, that reporters have a decisive influence in the field of foreign affairs seems to me preposterous. "You gentlemen," said President Wilson to the White House reporters, "are holding the balances in your hands. This unstable equilibrium rests upon scales that you control." Though it may have been true then, it is true no longer. The world of Wilson and the world of Johnson are as different as the two men themselves.

Reporters can irritate the President, divert him from his tasks, stir up his enemies, excite the public and force him to calm things down, and sometimes even make a persuasive point which he may modify policy to meet. But his power is at the center of action and we are at the edge, and my conclusion from this is fairly plain. We may be a nuisance, but we are not a menace. And the way power is running to the President, it would be unwise, I think, to concentrate too much on weakening whatever influence we have left.

VI

WHAT CAN BE DONE?

The Terrors of Competition

IN the State Department, the Foreign Service officers have a fable. The grasshopper, worried about getting through the winter, sought advice from the cockroach, who seemed to thrive on cold weather. The cockroach was sympathetic. On the night of the first frost, he suggested, find a warm spot back of a radiator in a bakery, turn yourself into a cockroach, and stay there happily until spring. "But how," asked the grasshopper, "do I make myself into a cockroach?" "Look," the cockroach replied, "I'm merely giving you policy guidance."

Most critics of the press give much the same kind of policy guidance: change and be saved, they say. Transform yourselves into something quite different from what you are; stop giving the customers just anything they want—any amusement, any violence, anything that sells beer or cosmetics—and give them instead the information they need to know to be good citizens in a democracy.

I agree, of course, with fostering a better-informed citizenry, but it is not much use advising grasshoppers to be cockroaches, or newspapers to be monographs on foreign affairs. The problem is to see whether, human nature being what it is, the people who sell newspapers can change to meet all these new responsibilities without losing the patronage of the people who buy and advertise in newspapers. Obviously, newspaper publishers cannot serve the national interest by going broke.

The death of the *New York Herald Tribune* in 1966 is only the most spectacular reminder of the economic problems of even the most illustrious of American daily newspapers. At the end, this paper, whose heritage stemmed from two of the finest dailies of the nineteenth century, and whose criticism of the arts, sports, and politics was as good as any in America, had a circulation of only about 100,000 among the more than seven million people living in the five boroughs of New York City. Despite its history, its reputation for originality and innovation, and its staff of nationally famous critics, it simply could not get sufficient advertising to keep going and is reported to have lost more than $20 million during the last ten years of its existence. Lectures on the ideal newspaper, therefore, are not likely to have much effect on newspaper publishers, for in the postwar years even *The New York Times* has made more money by owning a half-interest in a paper mill in Kapuskasing, Canada, and producing blank newsprint than it has earned by producing the best newspaper of record in the world.

This gives perhaps too gloomy a picture of the economics of American daily newspapers as a whole, however. The period of the great decline in the number of daily newspapers occurred between 1925, when there were 2,008 dailies, and 1945, when there were only 1,749. Actually, since 1945 and the rise of national television, the number of daily newspapers has remained fairly stable. Though they have not increased in proportion to the population, there are a few more now, mainly in the suburbs of the great cities, than there were in 1945.

Newspaper circulation and advertising have remained high despite the competition of television. More than sixty million papers are sold every day, and with the increase of higher education and the continued movement of the American people into large metropolitan areas where daily newspapers are most successful, there is every reason to believe that circulation demand will remain high. The main question is whether the newspapers will be able to keep their lead in advertising revenues over television, radio, magazines, and billboards in face of the steeply rising costs of newspaper labor, raw materials, production, and technical improvements.

Newspapers get about two-thirds of their operating revenues from advertising. Although they have continued to increase these revenues despite the competition of television, the rise is due largely to the fact that the economic prosperity of the postwar years has vastly increased the national investment in advertising of all kinds.

Nevertheless, the risks are high. All the modern instruments of communication in the United States are now caught up in a fierce competitive battle with one another and with the rising price of production. Everybody seems to be poaching on everybody else's preserve. The newspapers are now getting into the periodicals' field of "news significance"; the periodicals are invading the fields of both news and sociology, once dominated by the book publishers; the book publishers are producing "instant" paperback books on important news events; the television networks are bidding for the services of newspaper reporters, magazine writers, and historians; and all are engaged in a savage struggle for the advertising dollar. In this situation, it will not be very profitable to lecture publishers on their moral responsibilities unless it can be demonstrated that greater responsibility might produce greater prosperity. It is not a wholly new problem.

"To your request of my opinion of the manner in which a newspaper should be conducted, so as to be most useful," Thomas Jefferson wrote to John Norvell on June 14, 1807, "I should answer: by restraining it to true facts and sound principles only. Yet I fear such a paper would find few subscribers." Quite a few publishers have come to the same conclusion since then, and the competition for the citizen's time is increasing every year and tending to divert him from the most serious affairs.

The most insistent voices of America are now crying to the people night and day to think of other things: to buy and buy one more, to take in the Late Late Show, to join the Dodge Rebellion, or fly away from it all on Eastern Airlines—and on credit. We will only fool ourselves if we think we are going to compete on equal terms for the mass mind against the voice of the hawker, or bring about vast changes in the present ways of making, reporting, reading, and listening to the news. Some things, however, might be done in some important places.

The Advantages of Competition

Fortunately, some modern technical developments are forcing newspapers to be more responsible. I do not believe that journalists and officials in America are condemned by nature, like cats and dogs, to eternal hostility. There will always be times when the official will feel that it is his duty to conceal information and the reporter will believe it is his duty to publish it, but the area of conflict between them is narrowing and the area of cooperation is widening.

Newspapers are no longer the first messengers of the spot news. The radio deprived them of that function a generation ago. The noisy Horatio Alger urchin with a bundle of papers under his arm, shouting "Extra!" in the night, is a thing of the past. Though the radio and television reporters are competitive, they have never been as interested in "scoops" as the old newspaper reporters, and even now they are more concerned about sounding better and looking better than they are about going on the air first with some thumping disclosure.

Also, the television has deprived the newspaper of the great "picture" story. What poor scribbler can describe a political convention or the inauguration of a President as well as a television camera can capture such events? The modern newspaper is searching for a new role, or should be. That role, I believe, lies in the field of thoughtful explanation, which tends to make the reporter more of an ally of the government official than a competitor.

We are no longer merely in the transmitting business, but also in the education business. Actually, the mass communications of this country probably have more effect on the American mind than all the schools and universities combined, and the problem is that neither the officials who run the government nor the officials who run the newspapers, nor the radio and television news programs, have adjusted to that fact.

What Is "News"?

We are in trouble on the news side for a very simple reason: we have not kept our definition of news up to date. We are pretty good at reporting "happenings," particularly if they are dramatic. We are fascinated by events but not by the things that *cause* events. We will send five hundred correspondents to Viet Nam after the war breaks out and fill the front pages with their reports, meanwhile ignoring the rest of the world, but we will not send one or two reporters there when the danger of war is developing. Even if we do, their reports of the danger will be minimized, by editors and officials alike, as "speculation" and hidden back among the brassiere ads if they are not hung on the spike.

We can see now that the conditions of life in Cuba under Batista were big news, but we paid very little attention to what was going on there at the time. The *effect* was Castro and the risk of war with the Soviet Union; but the *cause* was the social inequality under previous regimes, many of them in cahoots with American commercial interests, and all this was largely ignored.

Unfortunately, there is not much evidence that the news organizations of the country have learned the lesson. Occasionally a television network or a large newspaper will send a team of reporters into the Dominican Republic or some other infected spot and do a useful study of the problems there. Most of the time, however, we rush from crisis to crisis, like firemen, and then leave when the blaze goes out.

I believe that we in the news business are going to have to twist ourselves around and see the wider perspectives of the news: the causes as well as the effects, what is going to happen in addition to what governments do. The foreign correspondence of American newspapers was based very largely on British models in general and on *The Times* of London in particular, but *The Times* had a very special function, which was not necessarily applicable to the United States. It was a kind of house organ for the British government Establishment. It concentrated on the news of what governments all over the world did: who was up and who down, who in and who out.

It is not governments that are transforming the world today, but the fertility of people, the creativity of scientists, the techniques of engineers and economists, and the discoveries of physicians. Almost all governments in the world today are merely rushing around trying to keep up with the consequences of what is happening outside their own offices. What the Roman Catholic Church does about birth control, for example, is probably going to be bigger news in the long run than what the American government does about foreign aid, which is overwhelmed each year by the staggering birth rate of the underdeveloped countries. The movement toward the unification of Europe did not start with governments but with private citizens like Jean Monnet. And it is being carried on by European businessmen—who like the larger markets and the fluidity of labor across national frontiers—rather than by governments.

Here again our profession, which prides itself on being up to date and is always shouting at governments to "keep up," is itself lagging behind the times. It has to go on covering "events," dealing with effects, and reporting the activities of governments; but, like the nation itself, its responsibilities have expanded. Ideas are news: see what John Maynard Keynes has done to our society with his ideas, what the conservatives backing Barry Goldwater did to the Republican Party and the balance of political power in America with their conservative revolt, what the Communists are doing to China with their savage ideology, what de Gaulle is doing to Europe with his patriotic yearning for national glory.

We are not covering the news of the mind as we should. Here is where rebellion, revolution, and war start, but we minimize the conflict of ideas and emphasize the conflict in the streets, without relating the second to the first. If the Secretary of Defense says, for the thousandth time, that the United States has enough hydrogen bombs on airplanes and submarines to wipe out both China and the Soviet Union, even after they destroy every major city in the United States, he is assured a big boxcar headline on the front page of every big-city newspaper in America and a prominent place on the Cronkite and Huntley-Brinkley shows. But if some thoughtful professor makes a speech demonstrating that the destruction of the human race can be avoided, he may easily be ignored even in his home town.

A Few Modest Proposals

What, then, can be done? Is there any way the flow of information can be increased, and the general understanding improved, without prohibitive costs?

I believe that the main hope lies in the expansion of the special correspondence in the large newspapers and news agencies, and of the special news events on the networks. All papers, agencies, and networks devote some time and money to serious studies of various social or political problems, but these "background" pieces tend to be irregular and are often cut down or squeezed out altogether by "hard news."

We are not likely to get much more serious correspondence in the big-city dailies until we stop making analytical articles compete for space with spot news. There is always more spot news, much of it trivial rubbish, than any paper can print. Nevertheless, an editor with two or three columns of serious correspondence on his desk is likely to fill up the paper with what happened "today" and leave out the special articles unless there is a specific policy on the paper to run several columns of this carefully prepared analysis every day. Most newspapers do print so-called "feature material." They do not make food recipes or fashions or comics compete every day with spot news for a place in the paper. They start with the proposition that they are going to publish these things each day for a special group of their readers. It would help if they did the same for their most thoughtful readers.

In the same way, the networks could help if they would set aside an hour each weekend in prime viewing time to review the important news of the week and put it into some historical perspective. Senator Fulbright stumbled into a fruitful pasture with his Viet Nam and China hearings. He brought together some of the best scholars of the nation and staged the first real debate on China policy since World War II. The purpose of the hearings was not to legislate but to educate. He merely noted: here is obviously a great question that needs to be discussed, and the television networks, after some scuffling in the corridors, took it from there.

The combination of Congressional hearings and network coverage has immense possibilities. Let the responsible committees of Congress explore the problems of population, of the Atlantic Alliance, of the balance of payments, of education and poverty—one great issue every month or so—and let the networks carry the principal parts of the testimony for an hour on the weekend. Again, we could easily lose by expecting too much. If this is to be done as a conscious effort to lift the level of attention on great issues, the networks will probably not carry the hearings live for hour after hour; but they might very well cooperate on an hour-a-week summary.

Ideally, the United States should have a radio and television service of special news and cultural events available on all sets and in all areas of the country. The National Educational Television network has made a beginning in this direction, but it does not have the scope or the funds to provide such a service for the entire nation. The Ford Foundation has suggested that the commercial networks, by using satellites for transmission of their programs, could save enough money to help finance an expanded educational television network, although it is probably a little idealistic to assume that the commercial networks will finance a competitor for the listening and viewing audience. No doubt, however, educational television can be expanded, by subscription or in some other way, so that there is a fuller flow of serious programming available to those families that wish to be informed as well as entertained.

Much more could also be done, through a nationwide educational television network and other ways, in the field of adult education on foreign affairs. This would require the preparation of the right kind of case studies on foreign-policy questions and their distribution to study groups in the churches, service clubs, and other nongovernmental organizations of the country. (We have seen how powerful the nongovernmental organizations of the United States can be in getting support for great acts of state like the Marshall Plan or the United Nations.) Though some of this goes on, more should be done.

The method of study is vital to its success. The problem is to present the great issues as a series of practical choices: let the people look at the alternatives as the President has to look at them and try at the end to decide among the hard and dangerous courses. We need simple case-study outlines containing, first, a statement of the facts of the policy question; second, a definition of one course of action, followed by arguments for and arguments against; and so on through definition of a second course, and a third and a fourth. The difficulty with the presentation of foreign-policy news to the people today is that it comes out a jumble of important and trivial things and personalities, so that the people cannot quite get clear the questions for decision, and end up either by giving up or by choosing up sides for or against the President. Even the Sunday newspapers might find room in their endless pages and sections for a syndicated case study of the issue of the month; and if not there, the foundations might take the project on.

If I may engage in a little heresy, it may be that news and analysis of news in a democracy are too serious to be left to newspapermen. The United States has been deeply involved in world affairs now for two generations. We have developed in the process a very large company of men and women in the universities, the foundations, international business, communications, and the government, who are well informed on international questions, some of them better informed on many subjects than any other people in the world. Unfortunately, not enough of these men and women are sharing with their fellow countrymen a great deal of what they know.

We are just beginning to develop a new class of public servants, who move about in the triangle of daily or periodical journalism, the university or foundation, and government service. These roving writers and officials are a growing and hopeful breed— McGeorge Bundy, Arthur Schlesinger, Jr., John Kenneth Galbraith, Theodore Sorensen, Richard Goodwin, and Douglass Cater illustrate the point—but much more of such cross-fertilization could be done.

It is not sufficient that these men write occasionally for the Sunday *Magazine* of *The New York Times*. The great opportunity of the daily newspaper is that it reaches people when they are paying attention. Galbraith can write a learned, amusing, and provocative book about his diplomatic mission in India, which would probably come out when everybody's mind was on the Congo or the sad decline of the New York Yankees, and if he was lucky, 50,000 people would read it; but if he took a day in the middle of the Indian-Pakistani war to analyze the conflict for the newspapers, he could have an attentive audience of easily twenty million.

We need more open pages, preferably next to the editorial pages, where the best minds of the world could give their analyses of current developments; where the vivid passages out of the best speeches and periodical articles and editorials of the world could appear; where we could find the philosophers worrying not about the particular bill of the day but about the issue of the decade. These could, if edited by thoughtful minds, be among the liveliest pages, bringing continuity to the daily newspaper and some sense of balance and history to contemporary events. The "Letters to the Editor" columns of many papers have been dominated by publicists and crackpots for years. We should be able to do better than that and make the open pages into an exciting forum for the exchange of ideas and even for criticism of the papers themselves.

Unfortunately, the American newspapers seldom encourage this kind of morning-after analysis by outsiders. The British do. H. G. Wells, G. B. Shaw, G. K. Chesterton, J. B. Priestley, to mention only a few, all started in the free-lance tradition of the British daily newspaper. "I am a journalist," Wells once declared late in his career. "I refuse to play the artist. If sometimes I am an artist, it is a freak of the gods. I am a journalist all the time and what I write *goes now*—and will presently die." He recognized the main point about journalism: it can get ideas to a mass audience at the fleeting moment when they are listening, and he preferred to use his energies to do that rather than to write tedious volumes for the few. "Better the wild rush of the Boomster and the Quack," he told Henry James in 1912, "than the cold politeness of the established thing."

The Competition for Brains

The need to bring the most thoughtful minds of the nation into the columns of the best of our daily newspapers is only a symbol of a more fundamental question about the philosophy and techniques of both newspapers and radio and television networks, namely, whether the newspapers and the networks can continue to follow the old habits of emphasizing what is bright, dramatic, contentious, and superficial, and still attract and hold the most serious and intelligent young men and women of the day in competition with other institutions. The universities, the foundations, the law, and the government are also looking for the same talents that make a successful reporter.

Thus, newspapers find themselves in a wholly new competitive position. Many of our most intelligent young men find it difficult to pass up the fellowships and scholarships that enable them to stay on in the universities, avoiding the military draft in the meanwhile. They do not have to put up with the endless grind of daily deadlines in order to write on the problems of their time. No doubt

many of these young men and women are fascinated by the conflicts of their generation and want to write about them, but attract-
ing them into daily reporting is not easy.

It is even more important to the future of newspapers and the
networks that these sensitive, intelligent young people find a
useful and sympathetic life in the reporting of contemporary
affairs than that the philosophic "outsiders" be encouraged to
write for the daily papers or talk on radio and television. Both
are important, but a newspaper and a network depend primarily,
like a baseball team, on who is on the field every day.

The best of American newspapers understood this in the 1950s
and 1960s. About that time they began to realize that they had
to reappraise their economic assumptions of the past and pay
their best reporters as well as they paid their best editors and
even some of their best executives. The reappraisal was not easy
for the owners of American newspapers because they had been
accustomed to the idea that reporters were satisfied with the
excitement of hobnobbing with political and commercial big-
shots, and would be satisfied with the wages of schoolteachers
or even parsons.

Since then, the publishers of the best newspapers have learned
that they are in a wholly new competitive situation for outstanding
talent. At least some of them have seen that the best of their
reporters were very much in demand by weekly news magazines
that made more money than newspapers; by Big Business, whose
public-relations activities were important enough to command
fabulous salaries; by the universities and foundations, whose
salary-level and work-year were more attractive than the routine
of day-to-day news reporting; and even by the Federal government, which concluded during the Kennedy Administration that
an effective newspaper reporter was competent enough to be a
good Assistant Secretary of State or Defense or even an ambassador of the United States at a higher salary than even the most
prestigious newspapers would normally pay.

Such recognition made a big difference, but the traditional
editors of the newspapers, oriented to the spot news of the day,

proved to be more of a problem for these reflective and analytical young men than the newspaper auditors. The reporters were looking for time and space to probe into the deeper meaning of the news. The editors were looking—not always, but a good deal of the time—for the main facts in a hurry. It would be wrong to say that the news editors were indifferent to detailed analysis of important stories, or that the new breed of intelligent reporters was uninterested in being first with the news or insensitive to the editors' problem of getting quick copy to the composing room in time to meet the pressing deadlines and railroad and airline schedules of the modern newspaper. But the preferences of the spot-news editor and the younger analytical reporter were different; and this was even more true of the editor and the reporter in the radio and television business, where a thoughtful reporter might gather a major story on some development in United States–Chinese relations and be told to present it in no more than forty-five seconds.

The whole point will be lost if we merely condemn the news editor. On a big city newspaper, he has to deal with a million words a day that pass through the office and select from them about 100,000 words for publication. Obviously, he cannot read the 100,000 words and, in most cases, not even the 10,000 that go into the major stories of the day. Thus he falls back most of the time on the old practice of printing the popular and cutting the rest to fit the limited space he has, which brings him into almost daily conflict with the reporter, who naturally thinks that nothing in the world is so important as the details of the beautiful story he has composed and finds mangled in the paper the following morning.

If I dwell on this point at the hazard of being tiresome, it is only because, first, the conflict of approach and philosophy must be resolved if the newspaper is to attain the level of intellectual excellence it needs in order to compete in the future; and second, the dominant role of the technicians in our newspapers is so typical of the crisis of leadership in so many American institutions today. John W. Gardner, formerly President of the Carnegie

Corporation in New York and now Secretary of the Department of Health, Education, and Welfare in President Johnson's cabinet, has touched on these problems of the specialist, the technician, and the philosopher in the wider context of American life.

"One of them," Gardner wrote, "is that it is nobody's business to think about the big questions that cut across the specialties— the largest questions facing our society. Where are we headed? Where do we want to head? What are the major trends determining our future? Should we do anything about them? Our fragmented leadership fails to deal effectively with these transcendent questions.

"Very few of our most prominent people take a really large view of the leadership assignment. Most of them are simply tending the machinery of that part of society to which they belong. The machinery may be a great corporation or a great government agency or a great law practice or a great university. These people may tend it very well indeed, but they are not pursuing a vision of what the total society needs. . . . One does not blame them, of course. They do not see themselves as leaders of the society at large, and they have plenty to do handling their own specialized roles. Yet it is doubtful that we can any longer afford such widespread inattention to the largest questions facing us."

This is a perceptive and apt description of the leadership not only of American government but of American newspapers and networks today. In general, the men who select and display the news in newspapers, and plan and allocate the assignments and the time for news and special events on radio and television, are not thinking about "the society at large" but about the competition; they are "tending the machinery" rather than attending to "the largest questions facing us." It is not that they are indifferent to the larger questions. They talk about them after working hours a great deal, and occasionally they plan special reports and special projects that deal with the effects of science, population growth, the rich third and the hungry two-thirds of the human family, automation and the unskilled worker, the races and the cities, food surpluses in America and starvation in South Asia. But "tending the machinery" is the main thing for most editors, and this usually means what happened or what somebody said today rather than whether it is important to the relationship of today to tomorrow.

These modest suggestions for broadening and deepening the flow of serious news in America are not really beyond the capacity of the big papers and stations; nor are they, in my view, against their long-range commercial interests. No doubt it would cost a bit more to give reporters time to investigate the causes of developing problems and set aside a few columns of space to keep their reports appearing regularly. But the gains would not be worthless. In this field we are better able to compete with radio and television than in the field of hot news. It is hard to psychoanalyze a President with a television camera or take a film of what hasn't yet happened. Also, if we let our reporters use their minds as well as their legs on serious inquiries and then print their findings, we will undoubtedly attract and keep more sensitive and perceptive men and women. At the same time, we would probably attract more and more of the intelligent young readers who are pouring out of our universities in an ever larger stream and are expecting from their newspapers a much more detailed and sophisticated account of world affairs.

To provide a fuller and more acute coverage is not a hopeless exercise by any means. The advertiser, at least in the large city, is no longer in a position to impose his views either of the President or of the Communists on the editor. I have never known a newspaper editor who was unalterably opposed to clear and vivid writing, though many of them tolerate some pretty shoddy stuff. There is a whole new generation of well-educated reporters who would welcome the opportunity to do more conscientious and careful work on major problems, and the more we get into this field of reporting, the less we are likely to be in conflict with officials.

The suggestion here is not that we try to make the daily American newspaper sound like a scholarly journal on affairs of state, that we put causes ahead of effects or ideas before facts, or the lonely professor's thoughts above the apocalyptic pronouncements of the Chairman of the Joint Chiefs of Staff, but merely that we give as much space to political ideas and social trends as we give, say, to new recipes on the women's page. It will not be easy to get a larger allocation of space or time for foreign and other serious news in the newspapers and radio and television stations, and it is silly to think that the reorganization of the political and social structure of Asia will ever get as much attention as sports or comics; but maybe a few papers and a few stations in the big cities might do better.

A little more self-analysis and a little less self-admiration would not hurt our business. We need to question not only our old definitions of news and our allocation of space and time but also many other popular assumptions that have been accepted uncritically for much too long. For example, we have a very patriotic and even chauvinistic press on the whole, which is good in some ways but bad in others. The newspapers didn't help the country much, in my view, by taking a "my country right or wrong" attitude when Presidents Kennedy and Johnson began slipping into the war in Viet Nam. It is difficult to see how we can get a clear picture of the world as it is if we see it only from our own side, like a football game, and do not challenge the national assumptions that we can do almost anything anywhere in the world.

It was a jingoistic American press that whooped us into the Spanish-American War and then, having helped extend our commitments all the way to the Philippines, confirmed isolationism as the first article of faith. Officials, of course, tend to complain that we are not patriotic enough and that we are constantly criticizing their actions and providing propaganda for the enemy, which is true enough. But the opposite is worse. We will have to become more detached, more disinterested, more forehanded and farsighted if we are going to report accurately and criticize effectively in this kind of mixed-up world.

Greater detachment and impartial criticism probably mean that we are going to have to question the validity of the party-oriented newspaper, at least as far as party views of foreign affairs are concerned. Fortunately, the my-party-right-or-wrong habit is declining anyway, but why should it exist at all in the foreign field? In the first place, it is virtually impossible in America to know what a party's foreign policy is when the party is out of power. Yet many papers still look at the world from the viewpoint of the party, or some leader in the party, and this clearly adds one more subjective and perplexing consideration to the puzzle.

It is not clear to me why the modern newspaper should give its allegiance to any party's foreign policy. A newspaper may very well conclude today that this country badly needs a stronger opposition party and therefore argue for more Republicans in the Congress, but for an editor to support Johnson in Southeast Asia because he is the editor's party's man or back Goldwater because he is the titular head of the editor's party is putting party ahead of country and cheating the readers.

The press has one extremely important job to do. We must try to keep the issues for decision clearly before the people, a task which is not really being done in the present jumble of the average American newspaper or news program. There is, for example, a new kind of class war developing in the world today between the rich nations and the poor nations. It does not take much imagination to see the chaos ahead in international life if this gap between the white industrial nations and the nonwhite agricultural nations keeps widening. Yet the foreign aid bill in Washington runs into more and more opposition every year, and the debate on that bill tends to come over to the readers as a battle between the "bleeding hearts" and the "realists." Also, the debates in the U.N. Economic and Social Council are seldom reported, and the direct confrontations between the rich and poor nations at U.N. headquarters in Geneva are scarcely mentioned by press or radio.

What the Government Could Do

On the official side, too, some improvements are desirable and even possible. The attitude of the President toward the reporters is vital. If he regards them primarily as a problem and therefore tries to manipulate them, they eventually convey their suspicion and even hostility to the people. If, on the other hand, he regards them as an opportunity and tries to explain his problems to them, they can be a valuable educational force. It is the President, however, who has the initiative and the capacity to define the rules and set the tone of public discussion.

There has been a decline since President Roosevelt's day, for example, in the use of the informative Sunday evening fireside chat, which was often used to good effect by FDR to explain the background of his problems. Now the President is on the air more often, but with bits and pieces of information or with his argument when public opinion seems to be going against him. A revival of the calm philosophic talk or the quiet "conversation," which President Johnson does extremely well, could help keep the public mind on the larger questions and minimize the capacity of others to divert attention into narrow personal or petty political issues.

There has been a decline in recent years in the relations between the experts in the State Department and the reporters. The reason for this is that the experts know the President likes to dominate public announcements and are afraid that they might disclose something that would detonate his temper. Since this is not a thought that many officials contemplate with pleasure, they tend to hold back, and since the most useful information in this field usually comes not from the top leaders but from the men who brief the leaders, this chokes down a very valuable stream of information.

No government in history ever received such a torrent of information from abroad as the United States government does today. Not only the ambassadors in the capitals and the experts on agriculture, economics, and politics in the embassies, but also the consuls scattered throughout the world in major cities and towns inundate Washington every day with reports on every imaginable problem in their areas. A good deal of this reporting is interesting and unclassified and could help nourish the flow of information into the newspapers and periodicals of the nation, but it is not made available mainly because nobody thinks of making it available. The idea has grown up that all this official information "belongs to the government." Nobody is looking at it and asking, "Why should this *not* be put out?" They have lapsed into the habit of not even considering the possibility.

It should be possible for officials and reporters to do much better than they have done in discussing the problems and opportunities of their relationships. There is a great deal of chatter about it, of course, with the White House Press Secretary on the Presidential press plane flying between Washington and Texas. But all suggestions for more formal committees to analyze and correct obvious shortcomings, or, alternately, for the press to establish some way of correcting itself, have usually ended in useless vapor.

Proposals have been made for the formation of a press council, like the bar association, that could pass on the ethics of its members. But what do you do when Drew Pearson comes up with thousands of incriminating documents out of a Senator's private files: disbar him or give him the Pulitzer Prize?

"If there is ever to be an amelioration of the condition of mankind," John Adams wrote in 1815, "philosophers, theologians, legislators, politicians and moralists will find that the regulation of the press is the most difficult, dangerous and important problem they have to resolve. Mankind cannot now be governed without it, nor at present with it."

I am more hopeful. I believe that an increasingly educated electorate will provide a growing market for more serious papers and more serious radio and television. They will not drive out the bad, but they will supplement it for the thoughtful minority.

As to the trickery of politicians, that, in the long run will prove, I think, to be a self-limiting disease simply because the people will catch on. Meanwhile, the willingness of serious men and women to discuss the question and moderate it in practical ways may prove to be more successful than we can now foresee.

VII

THE SAVING
REMNANT

RUNNING through all these random observations is a paradox that needs to be defined and, if possible, explained. On the one hand, it appears that much is wrong, obsolete, false, and maybe even dangerous in the relations between the American people and their government in the field of foreign policy; and yet, on the other hand, the results of the system are not too bad.

In the first place, the record of the American people in adapting to new conditions since World War II is not merely remarkable but unprecedented in the history of democratic societies. Whatever the conflicts between past and present, between officials and reporters, between old traditions and new responsibilities, the central fact is that the United States has changed its policies fast enough to be an effective force in world affairs.

It has created a new balance of power in the world. It has abandoned its old traditions of isolation, low taxation, no military conscription, and laissez-faire capitalism; and in the process, it has helped remove the spirit of domination that stained national and international politics, even in the Western world, during the period before and between the two world wars.

This is a remarkable achievement, and it is a pity that the American press has been so preoccupied with Washington's shortcomings that it has paid so little attention to Washington's accomplishments, but that is another story. Mainly because of these changes, commitments, and sacrifices by the United States, the world has gone through more than a generation without a major world conflict, which is more than can be said of the scrambling and disastrous disorder of the generation between the two world wars.

On the basis of this record, it is tempting to conclude that somehow the startling facts of the age have been getting through to the majority of the American people—that maybe, after all, our network of communications has been effective, and therefore that all this tiresome analysis misses the point. There is something to this conclusion. Undoubtedly, there is an intuitive feeling among the American people today that the world has changed so much that fundamental changes of policy are necessary. The question is whether they really agree with the changes of policy that are being made, or whether, confronted by all the complexities and ambiguities of change, they have merely given up and are acquiescing in whatever foreign-policy changes the President of the day makes.

The gap between theory and practice in the conduct of foreign affairs is very great. We go on pretending that "the people know best"; that the President merely administers the will of the Congress; that the Senate is a trusted partner of the President, who really wants its advice as well as its consent; and that the press, radio, and television really know what is going on in this field and therefore serve effectively as "the watchmen on the walls." There is, of course, some truth in all this, though not so much as we pretend.

If we are honest about the whole matter, we are forced to concede that the reality of our affairs is usually quite different. The thoughtful citizen, confronted by the tangled conflicts of foreign policy and often by the elaborate camouflage of official announcements, is not deceived by the pretense that he knows what to do about the disorder of Asia or the mysteries of international finance. He is usually fascinated but baffled by the endless torrent of intractable issues.

"The private citizen," Walter Lippmann wrote in *The Phantom Public*, "has come to feel rather like a deaf spectator in the back row, who ought to keep his mind on the mystery off there, but cannot quite manage to keep awake. He knows he is somehow affected by what is going on. Rules and regulations continually, taxes annually, and wars occasionally remind him that he is being swept along by great drifts of circumstance.

"Yet these public affairs are in no convincing way his affairs. They are for the most part invisible. They are managed, if at all, at distant centers, from behind the scenes, by unnamed powers. As a private person, he does not know for certain what is going on, or who is doing it, or where he is being carried. No newspaper reports his environment so that he can grasp it; no school has taught him how to imagine it; his ideals, often, do not fit with it; listening to speeches, uttering opinions, and voting do not, he finds, enable him to govern it. He lives in a world which he cannot see, does not understand, and is unable to direct."

What is even more disturbing, many members of the House of Representatives and the Senate feel much the same way. Of course, they pretend in public, especially at election time, that they have great knowledge and shrewd insights about foreign affairs; but in private most of them concede that they are overwhelmed by work, poorly informed about many critical foreign-policy problems, and, except in very rare instances, unable to control the rising power of the President in his dealings with other sovereign states.

Moreover, it is difficult to argue, in a world of nuclear weapons and transoceanic rockets, that more rigid restraints should be put on the President. He has to be free to act on an instant's notice in defense of the nation, and sometimes even when the sentiment of the people and the Congress is against him. There was obviously no time, for example, for President Kennedy to wait for a Congressional debate when Soviet ships were at sea in 1962, carrying rockets for emplacement in Cuba.

Yet the Presidential decisions to mount an indirect invasion of Cuba in 1961 and to send, by stages, a vast expeditionary force to Viet Nam raise serious questions about the democratic control of a President's power to wage war. In theory, the people are sovereign; but in practice, they are confused and divided. In theory, the Congress can restrain the President by refusing to vote the money to carry on his policies, or by refusing to approve his requests for authority to wage war "as he deems necessary" when confronted by Communist subversion or aggression. But in practice, when these votes are requested publicly at the moment of crisis, the Congress must choose between supporting the President or helping the enemy; and on this ground, even if it has the gravest doubts about the wisdom of the President's proposals, it is bound to support him.

It is much easier in such a situation for the President to manipulate the Congress than to persuade it; easier to overwhelm the press with statements, pronouncements, propaganda meetings, private interviews, messages to the Congress, trips to Asia—an endless avalanche of activity which dominates the news—rather than to convince the press that the President is following a clear line of policy, and saying the same thing in private that he says in public. The cost of this successful technique of manipulation, however, is very high; the people want to understand and believe in the actions of their government, but do not really believe. The Congress is told that it is the "partner" of the President in these critical foreign-policy decisions, but knows that it is not. The press is invited everywhere, urged to report and criticize, but is given the forms of participation without really participating and condemned for the criticism it is invited to make.

Nevertheless, there are, I think, reasons for believing that these relationships will improve. The quality and quantity of education in the United States are steadily increasing. Although it is easy to get lost in philosophic contention over whether it is better to educate the mass or to educate the elite, the facts are fairly clear: whether you measure our educational system by quality or quantity, the level is rising at a spectacular rate, and this is bound, in time, to have a positive effect on both our communications and our government.

Also, the trend of the American people is toward centralization in cities, where newspapers are easily and quickly available. As the level of education and taste rise, the demand for serious analytical reporting is likely to increase. *The New York Times* is a commercial success in New York, not only because of its quality but because there are enough serious people in a community of more than seven million to provide a large and prosperous audience that attracts advertisers.

Publishers and network officials generally concentrate on enter-
taining rather than on informing their public, not because they
prefer to be superficial but because, in the past, entertainment
has been more profitable than information. No doubt this statement will continue to be true, but the serious minority is growing
and will be an increasingly influential and commercially powerful
element that may very well bring into being more serious papers
and even a serious and expanded national educational television
network.

When Matthew Arnold came to the United States almost a
hundred years ago, he gave a lecture in New York on his
philosophy of "numbers." Like Plato and the Hebrew prophets,
Arnold had little confidence in the judgment of the mass of the
people, but he believed in the growing power of the intelligent
minority or what he called "the remnant" that sought knowledge
and wisdom. Athens, with its 350,000 inhabitants, and the King-
dom of Judah with its million, each had its "remnant" of wise and
intelligent citizens, but the "remnant" failed in both places,
Arnold insisted, because it was too small.

"But you [Americans] are something more than a people of
fifty millions," he told his audience. "You are not merely a
multitude of fifty millions; you are fifty millions sprung from this
excellent stock, having passed through this excellent Puritan
discipline and settled in this enviable and unbounded country.

"Even supposing," he added, "that by the necessity of things
your majority must, in the present stage of the world, probably
be unsound, what a remnant, I say—what an incomparable all-
transforming remnant!"

Arnold's prophecy may have seemed overly optimistic in the
last quarter of the nineteenth century, but after a hundred years
of popular education it does not seem unreasonable today.
The American educated "remnant" is not only growing in size
and in wealth, but it is demanding and buying more serious
publications, traveling more in the world, and growing into a
large, critical, and effective voting constituency that both major
political parties have to take into account. In short, the "remnant"

is getting large enough to form a profitable market for publishers and an increasingly articulate and influential factor in public affairs.

When, therefore, we wonder how we are to reconcile democratic government with the need for swift executive action in the tangled and complex field of foreign affairs, the chances are that we shall have to rely more and more on this expanding educated minority of our people. The constitutional theory that "the people know best" in the foreign field has consistently been challenged ever since the Constitutional Convention. Later, Tocqueville questioned its validity, and Lord Bryce asserted long ago that public opinion was essentially in the hands of two classes of people, who in turn had to rely on an accurate and dependable flow of information.

"There are," Lord Bryce wrote, "the men who seriously occupy themselves with public affairs, whether professionally as members of legislatures or journalists or otherwise actively engaged in politics, or as private persons who care enough for their duty as citizens to give constant attention to what passes in the political world. These persons are, taken all together, an exceedingly small percentage of the voting citizens. It is they, however, who practically make public opinion. They know the facts, they think out, and marshal and set forth, by word or pen, the arguments meant to influence the public.

"The second class consists of those who, though comparatively passive, take an interest in politics. They listen and read, giving an amount of attention proportionate to the magnitude of any particular issue placed before them, or to the special interest it may have for them. They form a judgment upon the facts and arguments presented to them. Their judgment corrects and modifies the views of the first class, and thus they are, though not the originators, yet largely the molders of opinion, giving to a doctrine or a proposition the shape it has to take if it is to succeed. . . . In countries accustomed to constitutional government, and when not swept off their feet by excitement, such men have the qualities of good jurymen and deliver a sensible verdict."

If this reliance on "the educated remnant" was true when Bryce wrote in the 1880s, it is infinitely more true today, for while the distribution of information is faster and wider now, the issues are so much more complicated and range over so many fields where special knowledge is essential that only Bryce's two classes of opinion-molders are likely to try to form sound judgments.

The key question, as I see it, is whether the newspapers and the radio and televsion networks are paying enough attention to this particular group of their readers and viewers. I do not believe they are. They are paying more attention to them than ever before, but still not enough. A vast and exciting debate is going on today in every advanced country on the changing relationships of the individual to the state, of nation to nation, of the rich to the poor, of the supply of food to the rise in population. It is nothing less than a reappraisal of the human predicament after a series of scientific, political, and social revolutions unprecedented in all history. All this is mentioned, of course, from time to time in the news, but no serious editor or television producer would claim that it is reported in measure to its importance.

My hope is that the best elements in the press, in networks and government, in the schools, colleges, universities and the church, in business, commerce and finance will prevail over the worst, and create a "remnant," in Arnold's terms, that will have a dom-inant influence on our society. My fear is that the "remnant" will be divided, exhausted, and corrupted. The danger of this is very real.

In the press, the networks, politics, the church, the schools and universities, and in commerce, the pressures today are running in favor of the conformist majority that offers the popular and easy answers to our problems. So great are these pressures, and so alluring the rewards of conforming to them, that we see all around us the resignation and even the surrender of many of our very best men and women.

In every newspaper and network office there are reporters and editors who feel we are not really reporting the larger dimensions of our time, but mainly the brutality and contention and frivolity of our time. In every school and college and in the Congress and in the Executive, there is this same minority, dissatisfied with the difference between what is and what might be. Yet all these places are full of defeated men who have tried and failed, and decided in the end that it was easier to give in to the pressures rather than to stand and fight for their ideals.

This, I believe, is the real danger. The responsible government official and the responsible reporter in the field of foreign affairs are not really in conflict ninety per cent of the time. When they do their best work, they are allies with one another and with "the remnant" in the nation that wants to face, rather than evade, reality. Clever officials cannot "manipulate" reporters, and clever reporters cannot really "beat" the government. From both sides, they have more to gain by cooperating with one another, and with the rising minority of thoughtful people, than by regarding one another as "the enemy."

INDEX

COUNCIL ON FOREIGN RELATIONS

Officers and Directors
John J. McCloy, *Chairman of the Board*
Henry M. Wriston, *Honorary President*
Grayson Kirk, *President*
Frank Altschul, *Vice-President & Secretary*
David Rockefeller, *Vice-President*
Gabriel Hauge, *Treasurer*
George S. Franklin, Jr., *Executive Director*

Hamilton Fish Armstrong
William P. Bundy
William A. M. Burden
Arthur H. Dean
Douglas Dillon
Allen W. Dulles
Thomas K. Finletter
William C. Foster
Caryl P. Haskins

Joseph E. Johnson
Henry R. Labouisse
Walter H. Mallory
James A. Perkins
Lucian W. Pye
Philip D. Reed
Robert V. Roosa
Charles M. Spofford
Carroll L. Wilson

PUBLICATIONS

FOREIGN AFFAIRS (quarterly), edited by Hamilton Fish Armstrong.
THE UNITED STATES IN WORLD AFFAIRS (annual). Volumes for 1931, 1932 and 1933, by Walter Lippmann and William O. Scroggs; for 1934-1935, 1936, 1937, 1938, 1939 and 1940, by Whitney H. Shepardson and William O. Scroggs; for 1945-1947, 1947-1948 and 1948-1949, by John C. Campbell; for 1949, 1950, 1951, 1952,

1953 and 1954, by Richard P. Stebbins; for 1955, by Hollis W. Barber; for 1956, 1957, 1958, 1959, 1960, 1961, 1962 and 1963, by Richard P. Stebbins; for 1964, by Jules Davids; for 1965, by Richard P. Stebbins.

DOCUMENTS ON AMERICAN FOREIGN RELATIONS (annual). Volume for 1952 edited by Clarence W. Baier and Richard P. Stebbins; for 1953 and 1954, edited by Peter V. Curl; for 1955, 1956, 1957, 1958 and 1959, edited by Paul E. Zinner; for 1960, 1961, 1962 and 1963, edited by Richard P. Stebbins; for 1964, edited by Jules Davids; for 1965, edited by Richard P. Stebbins.

POLITICAL HANDBOOK AND ATLAS OF THE WORLD (annual), edited by Walter H. Mallory.

ATLANTIC ECONOMIC COOPERATION: The Case of the OECD, by Henry Aubrey (1967).

TRADE, AID AND DEVELOPMENT: The Rich and Poor Nations, by John Pincus (1967).

BETWEEN TWO WORLDS: Policy, Press and Public Opinion in Asian-American Relations, by John Hohenberg (1967).

THE CONFLICTED RELATIONSHIP: The West and the Transformation of Asia, Africa and Latin America, by Theodore Geiger (1966).

THE ATLANTIC IDEA AND ITS EUROPEAN RIVALS, by H. van B. Cleveland (1966).

EUROPEAN UNIFICATION IN THE SIXTIES: From the Veto to the Crisis, by Miriam Camps (1966).

THE UNITED STATES AND CHINA IN WORLD AFFAIRS, by Robert Blum, edited by A. Doak Barnett (1966).

THE FUTURE OF THE OVERSEAS CHINESE IN SOUTHEAST ASIA, by Lea A. Williams (1966).

THE CONSCIENCE OF THE RICH NATIONS: The Development Assistance Committee and the Common Aid Effort, by Seymour J. Rubin (1966).

ATLANTIC AGRICULTURAL UNITY: Is It Possible?, by John O. Coppock (1966).

COMMUNIST CHINA'S ECONOMIC GROWTH AND FOREIGN TRADE, by Alexander Eckstein (1966).

TEST BAN AND DISARMAMENT: THE PATH OF NEGOTIATION, by Arthur H. Dean (1966).

THE AMERICAN PEOPLE AND CHINA, by A. T. Steele (1966).

POLICIES TOWARD CHINA: VIEWS FROM SIX CONTINENTS, by A. M. Halpern (1966).

INTERNATIONAL POLITICAL COMMUNICATION, by W. Phillips Davison (1965).

MONETARY REFORM FOR THE WORLD ECONOMY, by Robert V. Roosa (1965).

AFRICAN BATTLELINE: American Policy Choices in Southern Africa, by Waldemar A. Nielsen (1965).

NATO IN TRANSITION: The Future of the Atlantic Alliance, by Timothy W. Stanley (1965).

ALTERNATIVE TO PARTITION: For a Broader Conception of America's Role in Europe, by Zbigniew Brzezinski (1965).

THE TROUBLED PARTNERSHIP: A Re-Appraisal of the Atlantic Alliance, by Henry A. Kissinger (1965).

REMNANTS OF EMPIRE: The United Nations and the End of Colonialism, by David W. Wainhouse (1965).

THE EUROPEAN COMMUNITY AND AMERICAN TRADE: A Study in Atlantic Economics and Policy, by Randall Hinshaw (1964).

THE FOURTH DIMENSION OF FOREIGN POLICY: Educational and Cultural Affairs, by Philip H. Coombs (1964).

AMERICAN AGENCIES INTERESTED IN INTERNATIONAL AFFAIRS (Fifth Edition), compiled by Donald Wasson (1964).

JAPAN AND THE UNITED STATES IN WORLD TRADE, by WARREN S. HUNSBERGER (1964).

FOREIGN AFFAIRS BIBLIOGRAPHY, 1952-1962, by Henry L. Roberts (1964).

THE DOLLAR IN WORLD AFFAIRS: An Essay in International Financial Policy, by Henry G. Aubrey (1964).

ON DEALING WITH THE COMMUNIST WORLD, by George F. Kennan (1964).

FOREIGN AID AND FOREIGN POLICY, by Edward S. Mason (1964).

THE SCIENTIFIC REVOLUTION AND WORLD POLITICS, by Caryl P. Haskins (1964).

AFRICA: A Foreign Affairs Reader, edited by Philip W. Quigg (1964).

THE PHILIPPINES AND THE UNITED STATES: Problems of Partnership, by George E. Taylor (1964).

SOUTHEAST ASIA IN UNITED STATES POLICY, by Russell H. Fifield (1963).

UNESCO: Assessment and Promise, by George N. Shuster (1963).

The Peaceful Atom in Foreign Policy, by Arnold Kramish (1963).

The Arabs and the World: Nasser's Arab Nationalist Policy, by Charles D. Cremeans (1963).

Toward an Atlantic Community, by Christian A. Herter (1963).

The Soviet Union, 1922-1962: A Foreign Affairs Reader, edited by Philip E. Mosely (1963).

The Politics of Foreign Aid: American Experience in Southeast Asia, by John D. Montgomery (1962).

Spearheads of Democracy: Labor in the Developing Countries, by George C. Lodge (1962).

Latin America: Diplomacy and Reality, by Adolf A. Berle (1962).

The Organization of American States and the Hemisphere Crisis, by John C. Dreier (1962).

The United Nations: Structure for Peace, by Ernest A. Gross (1962).

The Long Polar Watch: Canada and the Defense of North America, by Melvin Conant (1962).

Arms and Politics in Latin America (Revised Edition), by Edwin Lieuwen (1961).

The Future of Underdeveloped Countries: Political Implications of Economic Development (Revised Edition), by Eugene Staley (1961).

Spain and Defense of the West: Ally and Liability, by Arthur P. Whitaker (1961).

Social Change in Latin America Today: Its Implications for United States Policy, by Richard N. Adams, John P. Gillin, Allan R. Holmberg, Oscar Lewis, Richard W. Patch, and Charles W. Wagley (1961).